MW00465558

"A Profoundly Vulnerable Tap

Dr. Shokef's book, *The Promis*

of awe fused gently with welcomed recognition. The heart-stopping details shared from every aspect of her miraculous story of surviving a debilitating car accident and the long nonlinear journey of recovery she still is living is balanced by profound insights she took away from a simultaneous NDE (near-death-experience) while in the grips of the accident itself. Her lesson for us all to remember, if we choose, is that nothing else matters other than the pure Truth, Attentiveness, and Motion of LOVE. As a fellow survivor of several NDEs, I found great comfort and healing in reflecting upon my own experiences while delving into the vast insights of her own. Shokef is a skilled storyteller, and her palpable vulnerability is a loving invitation to the reader to explore your own self-healing via whatever 'classroom' life presents you, not only as a parent but as a being that is both human and spiritual. No matter who you are or what you've experienced, reading this book just might change your life if you're willing to receive the grace it promises to share."

— **Nanci Reed**, *Spiritual Teacher, Speaker, and Bestselling Author of the award-winning book Happily Ever Now*

"[...] *The Promise We Made* is such a special golden thread in both the spiritual and parenting book genres. Efrat doesn't try to give you just a cognitive understanding of Spiritually Aware Parenting, rather, she offers a beautiful trio of heart centered focuses. This trinity is composed of her own personal experiences around a Near Death Experience and her recovery, allegorical stories received in meditation to illustrate the spiritual growth and simple practices for you, the reader, to embark on the embodiment of the concepts being discussed. This means you don't read a chapter and then find yourself trying to force yourself to integrate what's being discussed. Rather, the stories and philosophies dance around you, so you can just allow them to flow through you, gently realigning you to a new state of being and consciousness.

It is rare to find a book that allows you to experience spirit rather than just read about it. [...] What Efrat has achieved with this book is create a testament to this journey, this inner dance between human contrast and the spiritual love that is ever flowing. She has offered, through her own experiences, insights, stories and profound tools, a roadmap for parents who feel called to something deeper within their relationship and life they are building with their families. Through the con_ cepts of Truth, Attentiveness, and the Motion of LOVE, she offers foundational cornerstones on how to build a spiritually aware family and an intuitive, heartfelt path to create them. [...] Having a guide like *The Promise We Made* gives you a steady pace to grow with, rather than the panic to "heal" in a rush. Tapping into the field of Love, remembering who you really are, creates just the right timing. The journey of the Spiritually Aware Parent can often feel isolating and confusing. This is yet another reason why *The Promise We Made* is such an important addition to any parent's library. It reminds you that while the journey is uniquely yours, there are others traveling it, right along with you. May your journey be blessed with love and the light of everything you really are."

— ***Christina Fletcher***, *Author, Teacher, and Healer*

"Explore the spiritual dimensions of parenting through this heartwarming memoir, offering profound insights and practical advice for living with greater awareness, compassion and connection with our children."

— *Jacob Cooper*, LCSW, *Bestselling Author of Life After Breath and The Wisdom of Jacob's Ladder.*

"[...] *The Promise We Made* goes beyond the typical parenting guides, delving into the often-neglected realm of spirituality in parenting. Efrat's exploration of the soul agreements between parents and children is a unique and enlightening perspective. Through her personal story, she unravels the essence of parenting, asking profound questions about our roles as mothers and fathers. Her journey to become the mother her children chose unfolds as a powerful testament to the transformative potential within each parent-child relationship. The book articulates three primary soul promises—Truth, Attentiveness, and the Motion of LOVE—universal agree_ ments that resonate with every parent. Efrat masterfully guides readers through the importance of embodying truth, fostering attentiveness, and embracing the motion of love for mutual growth and transformation. Efrat's writing is not just a guide; it is an invitation to embark on a spiritual journey of self-discovery and conscious parenting. Her words are filled with wisdom, compassion, and a deep understanding of the sacred bond between parents and children. *The Promise We Made* is a light for parents seeking to bring spirituality into their parenting journey. Efrat Shokef Ph.D. has written an enlightening story that not only shares her personal story but also serves as a guiding light for parents navigating the sensitive terrain of raising children connected to their essence. I wholeheartedly endorse this book, knowing it has the power to create a positive ripple effect in the lives of families worldwide."

— *__Marla Hughes__ M.S. Author, Spiritual Practitioner, Seeker*

"[...] *The Promise We Made* is full of beautiful truths, insights, and practical exercises to help you integrate the lessons she shares with beautiful stories at the beginning of each chapter that help you connect to her personal story in your own way. Sometimes, when our world feels like it's falling apart, it opens us to a new dimension, giving us an opportunity to align with our true and correct path, and this book and Efrat's story is a beautiful example of how struggle, uncertainty, and challenge can be threaded through with gratitude, acceptance, and love. I finished reading this book with a full heart and a reminder that we are all LOVE, that we are connected through love, and that we get to choose how we show up each day through what Efrat refers to as soul moments. These moments occur every day and offer us a choice, an opportunity to align more deeply with our soul's purpose here on Earth. This book is for every parent and every adult child who has ever wondered if they're doing it right, what their purpose is, or why life throws us curve balls. It is for those who wonder what the point of our challenges are and what is beyond this world."

— *__Aypril Porter__, Bestselling Author of Parenting the Child You Have: Re-Imag ining the Parent-Child Relationship Through the Lens of Human Design.*

"This book is an absolute gem of life wisdom. Through her personal story of becoming re-aligned with soul after the challenges of a near-death experience, Efrat Shokef explores what it means to love fully in a way that honors our true spiritual origins. She skillfully guides readers to embrace our own journey with authenticity, create space for "soul moments", and enable those we love to truly be who they are. This touching and inspiring story elevates our understanding of love through one of its purest forms - a mother's deep love for her children."

— *Liz Beachy Gomez*, *Founder of Ewassa and Author of the award-winning book: From the Depths of Creation: A Nature-Based Path to Healing.*

"This thoughtful book takes us on a sacred journey to becoming a spiritually aware parent, a journey we may have not realized we longed to embark upon. After a Near Death Experience, the author was guided along a path of understanding and ultimately teaching spiritual parenting. The path forward for parents is illuminated by lovely and meaningful exercises to help us find our own undiscovered wisdom we can tap into to assist each soul in our care to grow into its full potential. Whether parenting small children or grown ones, there is something here for everyone. I highly recommend this profound deep dive into the sweetness of sacred parenting."

— *Karen V Johnson*, *J.D, M.P.H, M.P.I.A, Shaman and Silver Nautilus award-winning Author of Living Grieving: Using Energy Medicine to Alchemize Grief and Loss.*

To Yaara, Dafna, and Hadas

THE PROMISE WE MADE

Three Universal Soul Promises We Made to Our Children

EFRAT SHOKEF PhD

Blooming Sage
Publishing

Cover Art and Design by Claire Sieverts

Author Photo by Magdalena Deffner

Paperback ISBN: 978-965-93181-0-0

ebook ISBN: 978-965-93181-1-7

Blooming Sage Publishing

Contents

An Invitation

DEAR READER, THIS IS the book I wished I had when life invited my family and me to embark on a journey, stormy and greater than we thought we could withstand. I was severely injured in a car crash and had a Near Death Experience (NDE) that awakened me to the many layers and beauty of our world. All NDEs come to teach us about life, and mine invited me to look at a clear mirror reflecting the gaps between who I am, the numerous limited views I held, and what was possible.

For months, while healing, I could not participate in the care-taking of my daughters. My prayer to be their mother sent me on a quest for the essence of motherhood – an archetype in itself. I searched for an essence that is not dependent on anything – unconditional parenting and love. An essence that would define me as their mother, not by what I do or don't do.

I found this essence in a forgotten promise of love. I discovered profound yet straightforward understandings of our spiritual (beyond religion) nature and what our children ask from us: universal sacred agreements we all make with our children. These understandings transformed me and changed my relationship with my daughters and our whole family. Now, over ten years later, they guide many of my clients – fellow parents, hearing their hearts' call to know more about the spiritual essence of our sacred relationship with our children.

This book offers a grounded perspective on spiritual (beyond religion) parenting, viewing spiritually aware parenting as the act of guidance and care for souls arriving on Mother Earth. Spiritually-aware parenting invites us to ask, what are the soul agreements we make with our children? And hence, what conditions does each soul need to grow its physical vessel and spiritual conduit so that it can walk the path it asked for, manifesting its soul's journey here on Earth?

My many injuries invited a complete physical reorganization. The NDE was an invitation to embrace and develop my ability to see and sense beyond our physical senses. It was an invitation to a space of luminous love, where I started remembering who

I am and could explore the essence of parenting, which I share with you in this book. This is the parenting guidance, spiritual and sacred, I looked for when I came out of the eye of my storm.

The parables at the beginning of each chapter are mythical stories that offer healing. I invite you to read them with your heart and let them touch your heart like they touch mine.

The book includes many tools and exercises I used in my healing journey, which have since helped many other parents I work with. You can download them as a workbook, including audio versions of the meditations offered, at www.efratshoke f.com.

I hope that the parables, tools, exercises, and questions brought up within the book will spark your thoughts and then your heart. Or maybe your heart first, and then your thoughts – offering an additional way to look at your relationships with those wonders that make you a parent, guiding you to arrive at a new way to love, even in the most challenging of life's journeys.

Efrat

Before

ONCE, BY THE RIVER of time, sat a mother and her child. They enjoyed a day together by the streaming water, sparkling from the sun above. They unfolded a picnic blanket and took some fruit and water from a basket they had brought for their outing. Then they lay on their backs, enjoying the surrounding grazing land and wildflowers. They searched for shapes in the light, white clouds gracefully flowing over their heads. They played. They laughed.

While looking at the streaming water, the child, pointing to the river, suddenly asked, "What direction is the water going?"

The mother, surprised at his question, looked where he was pointing. Then they both looked to the right and the left, trying to *make sense of the water's direction. Is it going downstream or up?*

After a long moment, the child looked at his mother with big, amazed eyes and said with contentment, as if he had just discovered what he always knew, "It goes in both directions!"

His mother looked again and nodded. "Indeed it does," she said, feeling a sense of relief, as if she, too, always knew that.

They stood there, watching the motion of the river. Attentive to the directions it takes. Looking at the flow going down, and also up, and how, at places where the individual drops within it are unsure, they blend, creating a whirlpool, until they each know the direction they need to take at that particular moment. The child and his mother smiled. They returned to their picnic blanket with a shimmer of gratitude. Together remembering what their hearts always knew.

Life is about surprises. Sometimes filling us with unexpected joy and, at other times, inviting us to face them. With all their might, reverence, and astonishing forces of nature, dancing to their rhythm, cycle, and flight. Weaving. Weaving their threads into our human life. And within their flow, we humans can only stand breathless before their magnificent force. Washing us away from one self to another, taking us through whirlpools and whirlwinds, spitting us out on new shores, never to return. Inviting us to awake and live our lives with attentiveness to the truth that walks in our hearts. To live our life by choice.

It was four days before an event that transformed my life and my family's life. Like an emerging thunderstorm on a sunny day, heard lightly from a distance. Almost unnoticed. It was morning, and I was tidying up our small house. My husband took our toddler to daycare. Our twins had recently turned one, and I had invited some other mothers and babies from our community for a small celebration – a mother's celebration of surviving a very challenging, sleepless year.

I was thirty-five, a mother to three little ones: a toddler who was then three years and four months old and thirteen-month-old identical twin girls. I had recently finished my Ph.D. in social-organizational psychology and a short post-doc funded by a Fulbright Scholarship. I was home with my daughters and worked part-time, doing research and teaching academic courses. I felt I was managing better and better the joint dance of our growing family. Learning to rest between steps, finding the daily motion, and breathing into it.

Around 9:30 am, our friends started to show up. Our small kitchen table began to fill with little dishes of food: homemade granola in a glass jar, just-made cookies, a fresh-smelling loaf of bread covered with a kitchen towel to keep it warm, home-made jam, tahini, freshly cut avocado, and salads. The food was placed – and people helped themselves to it – with no apparent order. Our kettle whistled, and the mugs were filled with hot coffee and tea. A few of them were placed somewhere high, where the babies would not be able to reach them. Most of them stayed full for the rest of the gathering.

We formed a circle, inviting each mother to share her perspective on motherhood and its meaning to her. My twins were crawling within the circle with their friends, coming to me to nurse every few minutes, and going back to their exploration of the other babies and mothers in the circle surrounding them.

I looked forward to my turn to share. As the last in the circle, I had plenty of time to consider my words, to think about my gratitude to the many mothers in this group, aiming to reflect on the twins' first year. As in the unforeseen curves of a flowing river, once it was my turn to share, my words were all lost. No sound came out of my mouth. After a quiet moment, all I managed to whisper was:

"I want to be their mother."

I choked on my breath. Confounded in my place. I was completely surprised by my own words. *Why did I say that? The words I had planned to share were completely different. Words of gratitude and expansion. Why would I want to be their mother? I already am, aren't I?*

A few seconds later, the babies continued with their play, sounds, and needs. One mother reached up to her cup of tea placed on the shelf above her, spilling half of it on herself. One of the babies needed a diaper change, another to nurse, general chatting took over, and some mothers got up to grab some food from the table. The friend to my right, a little concerned, tried to ask if I was okay. I had no answer. I did not understand the words I lost and the words that came. Was that a slight, tiny, soft wind hinting at the coming storm? Later that day, I wrote it in my journal, and the full days ahead swept it away.

Now, over ten years later, I know in my heart that it was a prayer that came from deep and unfamiliar parts of my soul, from a place within me I was scared to recognize and afraid to connect to. I was unknowingly asking; I was unknowingly praying to remain here on Earth with my family, praying to continue being a mother to my three beautiful babies, to live our life to its fullest.

Four days passed without notice. I don't remember much of them. They were typical days, full and happy. Days spent with our three daughters, friends, and neverending housework. These days were also full of many slightly unnoticed, as if negligible, small moments of discomfort. Moments of crashing tired next to the piles of laundry. Moments of closing my eyes for two or three minutes whenever I could, barely managing to open them again. Moments of gazing through the window in the hopes of a short quiet moment. Moments in which I was not sure what was right, even in the management of small everyday events. Should we go to the playground or stay home? What should we prepare for dinner? Moments of considering when and at what intensity I should go back to work. Do I want an academic career and to continue teaching? If I work only a few hours a week, which of the many paths I was fortunate to be trained in do I want to follow? Should I maybe change the focus of my professional activity? As much as our lives seemed to be getting into order, finding the rhythm of their breath, and although I had so much to be grateful for, I was not fully present or happy in my home, with my daughters, with myself.

Moments of discomfort can be influential teachers if you listen to them. I did not. I dismissed these moments with many excuses, the leading one being that I was a mom to three babies. A good reason, but inattentive to my heart calling from within me. These small discomforts were a delicate reflection that there was something in my life that was not aligned. With who I am. With who we all were as a family. I left these moments almost unnoticed and completely unattended. After all, everything seemed promising. We felt we were standing on stable land. Then, the event waiting around the corner upended our lives.

The morning of January 6, 2011 was a peaceful Thursday morning. Rain was lightly falling. The sun was touching the drops, making everything sparkle. As on other Thursday mornings, the only morning I was teaching at the time, I dressed nicely, got my toddler ready for her day, we all had breakfast, and I nursed the twins together. My mother came to watch them, both happily crawling directly into her arms. My husband walked our toddler and me to the car, helping her in. On the way to her daycare, we sang, welcoming the rain, delighting together in the drizzle washing the air around us. When we arrived, I sat with her for a few minutes. I had plenty of time to get to the college campus in Jerusalem for my class.

We hugged and kissed goodbye. I was to pick her up on my way back.

Tiny raindrops were pounding on my car window; the sun came out for a few seconds and disappeared. I remember a long wait until I could turn left into the main road. Long, yet calm. Then, less than 500 meters after I left the village, while joyfully enjoying the view of the showered trees and the sparkle of the raindrops on their leaves, a deep, unfamiliar *boom* awakened all my senses.

It came.

Silence

Stillness

Calmness

Peace

After the *boom*, I heard nothing. Not even the birds continuing to sing on the large old carob tree growing by the road.

The 9:00 am radio news reported, "There was a serious car crash on Highway 44. Two cars were involved. Two women were injured, one severely. The road is blocked to traffic in both directions." By the 11:00 am news, the road was open to traffic. My shoe was left lonely on the roadside by the old carob tree.

Silence.

Stillness.

A glorious quietness, and the delicate sound of faraway bells.

Light.

Bright and warmly intense. Radiant, yet not dazzling.

The most magnificent place I have ever been to.

Immediately after the crash, I felt myself expanding and hovering in soft, white, shimmering surroundings. A feeling I wish I could adequately describe. But words cannot capture the feeling that still, years later, expands my cells. An experience stored not in my mental memory but in the deepest essence of my physical and energetic being. The stillness was magnificent. Tranquil, serene, perfect, and enveloping as only true silence can be. No sound but the sound of inner music and distant soft bells. Waves of soft white light were moving delicately around me. Like feather clouds, yet much softer. A sense of pure love was enveloping me, sliding by my luminous skin, bubbling into my being, reminding me what we are all made of. I felt peace as I never had before.

Where was I? It was incredible, breathtaking in its beauty. It was unlike anywhere I consciously remembered, yet I knew I knew this place and had been here before. It was both new and familiar. A place outside of linear time and space as we know them here, and our Earthly vocabulary is not sufficient for describing it. While there, I was unaware that I was not in my physical body, the one I walk within this lifetime. Nor did I realize that my physical body was a mess. I did not know I was in the midst of a near-death experience (NDE). My Earthly identity, family, friends, and children were not on my mind either. It's not that I forgot them. But for those moments, my Earthly consciousness was not active. I had no sense of self. I was where I was, in the now of those moments. A magnificent present. Nothing else had any significance. Not in any conscious awareness. It was a familiar, new, fabulous, luminous space to be in. The most beautifully enveloping, calm, and loving place I have ever visited. It felt like home. A place to stay in. Forever.

The surrounding light was strong and pure, yet its brightness did not dazzle as it would on Earth – but that is an understanding that came later. It felt like this light was bubbling into me and informing every piece of my being. My inner sense expanded. I felt intact, complete, and whole. Whole in every aspect of my being. I was enveloped by the core force of our universe – LOVE. It was all so pure that, within me, I knew there were no questions. This was it – the essence of it all. The core center of our beings, as individuals, as one. As Earth, as the universe and its multiple dimensions. I felt deep acceptance. Self-acceptance and self-love merged with the acceptance and LOVE of everything. I was part of and one with all. Within my being and down to my cells, I gradually recognized that the light bubbling into me was bringing LOVE. Was LOVE. Until I felt that I myself was LOVE.

I remember I was floating forward and sensed I was not alone. A few vague beings were floating in the same direction that I was. At the same time, many luminous beings were floating slowly in the direction others and I had come from. Some seemed to be very long and different, and others had more human features. Their movement was soft. As if dancing just above an apparent luminous ground.

Slowly, I felt myself floating toward those luminous, dancing, floating beings. Some of them, in small groups, accompanied the others coming with me. From the side, they looked like happy, enveloping gatherings. All of the arriving souls were happily welcomed back home. Once they met, they moved forward together. It was touching to see the mutual recognition and embracement – the meeting of hearts.

I floated forward until I couldn't continue. I felt I had reached an invisible boundary the others had crossed, but I could not. Everything around me was so still and beautiful. I felt like I was me in my essence, absorbing the LOVE bubbling in, and it did not matter that I was not moving forward like the others. At the time, I did not understand that these were all souls who had just emerged from their physical bodies – died – and were now being welcomed by their guides and soul families.

After a timeless time, a single figure floated towards me from that invisible border I could not cross. The closer the single glowing, luminous figure came, the stronger the sense of familiarity grew. It looked like the father of my father, who had passed away from cancer when I was nine years old. He did not look like I remembered him, yet he did. It seemed like yesterday. We did not talk. Just looked into each other's eyes. Talking through our hearts, knowing all was well. Signaling how much we love one another. This wordless communication strengthened that feeling already bubbling into me that I was LOVE too, and I am always loved as I am.

My grandfather invited me to stand by him on a shimmering white stone balcony and view the universe. He was there to make the most out of my visit to the realm of LOVE. To be a guide and open my heart, mind, cells, and whole being to the possibilities and knowledge of our universe. In retrospect, I sometimes wonder if it was indeed my grandpa's soul coming to guide me, or if it was my luminous guidance, always watching over me, that embodied his image to ease our meeting in those sacred moments.

It felt like the balcony was standing in place and that, in parallel, the areas below were flowing. And yet, it could have also been the other way around. We observed the Earth. Its people. Some in cities. Some living on distant mountaintops. Some listening to their hearts. Others swept away by human noise. Often, they create a pool of sorrow, pain, and loss around them, drowning in their own tears. My grandfather, my guide, was expanding my understanding of humanity. It was so rich. So magnificent. At times also extremely sad. We humans so often forget our pure essence. I was shown so many different places. So many dimensions of life. So much beauty, so many alternatives and choices.

After what seemed to be days but was only a few minutes in Earthly time as we know it, my grandfather told me, "This is not your time. You must go back now," adding with his eyes the urgency of returning to my body.

He had shown me all that I needed to see. All that I could absorb at that time. I was there, in what some would refer to as an altered state, outside of time and outside of space, for almost as long as was possible. The way he urged me to return to my body, I understood that staying in this serene, beautiful place of LOVE – meaning not coming back to my body, my family, Earth – was not an option. I was not asked or given a choice; I was to return, immediately. This knowing was within me, just as it had been given.

In the flip of a second, I was floating backward, departing from my beloved grandfather with my distancing eyes. Then I was pulled down, and I fell into my own physical body.

Boom.

Returning to my body was another crash. I was overwhelmed with the pain sending signals from my leg, arm, neck, back, and especially my belly. The pain was tremendous. It was stronger than the one intense pain I was familiar with, of birth contractions at their peak. It was so strong. I could not breathe. I could not even cry.

"Were there babies in the car with you?" I vaguely heard someone ask.

I did not understand why someone would ask me about babies in my car. I did not see any cars around me in this luminous, serene space of LOVE.

"Were there any babies with you?" The unfamiliar voice asked again. I tried to answer, but he did not seem to notice.

"Were there any children with you? Talk to me," he kept repeating.

But he did not seem to hear any of my responses. I was coming and going in and out of my body. Not managing to bear the pain, confusion, smells, and noise of ambulances and paramedics, watching them from above carefully breaking my car door to remove me, while putting out a fire that had started in its front.

A little over a year after the car crash, my husband and I gratefully met the man who was by me, talking to me. In our meeting, he told us that he did not see the crash happen but arrived immediately after it and that he was afraid these were my last moments. My eyes were rolling back in my head, and I was hardly breathing. The ambulance driver told him to keep talking to me. He saw the bases of the click-connect infant car seats in the back seat and repeatedly asked if I had any babies with me. I came back and drifted away. He said that he thought it was several stressful minutes until I suddenly opened my eyes and clearly stated that my daughters were not with me and gave him my home number, asking him to call my husband. After that, I drifted away again. For me, those few minutes of our Earthly linear time seemed much longer. It felt like days. So much had happened.

As soon as my husband got the call, he left everything. He quickly told my mother that he would update her, did not even kiss the twins, and drove to the location of the crash, which was less than ten minutes from our house. He drove on the road's shoulder, trying to pass the traffic jam the car crash had created, until he could no longer proceed. He parked on the side and threw the keys to a friend stuck in the traffic jam (who did not know it was me ahead), asking him to bring his car home. Then, he managed to make his way through the police and paramedics to me.

By then, I had already received strong painkillers, reducing the pain but not removing it. He reached his hand through the paramedics, putting it on my forehead, saying to me, "I am here."

I could let go. He was there, and I trusted him to take care of whatever needed to be taken care of. I surrendered to the painkillers and drifted away. He was shocked, yet supportive to me as only he could be at that time. Simply with me. As he always is, from this time, from others, from eternity.

A helicopter was on its way, and the ambulance transferred me to a location where it could land and take me to the hospital. Somehow, my husband convinced the helicopter crew to let him join them instead of trying to drive. Later, he shared that the other woman from this story, my fellow in the car crash, wounded too, was also with us on the helicopter.

The painkillers managed to numb me. I vaguely heard the talk around me but could not repeat it even a moment later. I recall the paramedic asking for my husband's permission to cut off my dark red wool coat so that they could stabilize my left arm. I painfully remember the tilting of the wheeled stretcher into the ambulance, and then the noise within the helicopter. Yet mostly, I was not there.

I had severe internal bleeding in my abdomen and was losing blood. Upon reaching the hospital, I was immediately taken into an emergency operation. For the first few days, I was put into an induced coma, anesthetized in the intensive care unit. Not clearly here. Not yet dead. The doctors' prognosis was very vague. They avoided making any optimistic promises that my family would hang onto. They did not say I would live, and they did not make any prediction about my physical future or the expected length of my hospital stay.

I hardly have any memories of my physical existence during these days. My body was lying dismantled in the intensive care unit, blipping noises all around it, my abdomen with an open wound. My essence, my soul, was not there, but unconsciously returning to the comforting sense of pure LOVE and acceptance. Escaping from my nonfunctioning body, I was drawn to the serene, peaceful, accepting, and still memories I had just experienced in what I would later learn was an NDE and a visit to the dimension of cosmic LOVE.

After a few days, the physicians lowered the anesthesia, and I was invited to return. I opened my eyes for a few seconds and then fell back into unconsciousness. I woke up not knowing what had happened yet fully accepting the situation, as if some profound, unconscious understanding was leading me. I realized I had been in a car crash only after being told so. I did not consciously know I had experienced an NDE. I was unable, at the time, to share in words what I had experienced, felt, and was taught, but I felt it in my cells. I knew within me that beyond the breaking of my body, something significant and different had taken place. Something I had no words for.

Something that was beyond my mind's ability to comprehend. Even for myself. I was both broken and whole at the same time.

Receiving strong painkillers, I did not feel most of my body. I recall very few memories of those days: a friend coming into the room, me opening my eyes for a brief moment, my mom by my side, the friend showing me a necklace she had brought me, me smiling in gratitude and drifting back to sleep. Another friend standing by me, telling me she sent my husband to the hospital shops to get himself something to eat and buy me a toothbrush. A nurse washing me for the first time, taking pieces of glass out of my red hair. Me crying in pain from every tilt and move. The first time I was taken with a lever into a chair, to have me sit a little, it was so painful that I cried to the nurse to get me back to the bed. And the drawing of a giant purple flower on the ceiling of the intensive care room.

After a few more days, I was transferred to the surgical department and was there for another month and a half. My family and close friends did not leave me alone for a moment, blessing me with their love. During the days, it was mostly my husband or my mother that stayed by my hospital bed. Other family members and some very close friends took shifts mainly at night. I still gratefully keep a bunch of felt flowers made by some friends, full of their blessings for my healing.

When my mother and husband were not with me, they were at our home, taking care of our little girls. Life at home was displaced, much like my own. I was told only much later that my twin babies cried for me in the first two weeks, especially during the nights. Either my husband or one of my parents, who moved into our house on the day of the crash, was always with them. I, their mother, who had been with them almost every minute and definitely during every night, had disappeared. Nursing was suddenly stopped. My breast discharged milk mixed with blood at the hospital, far away from them.

On the first night, my husband left me with my brothers. He had to get home to our daughters so that they could at least see him. Later, he shared that when he came in, our toddler was on the couch. My father, her grandfather, was reading her a story. She looked up. My husband washed his hands, changed his shirt, and then sat by her. He said she hugged him like never before. What did she understand?

The beautiful community we live in reached out and cooked for us for months. Friends with little ones the same age as mine came over to our house so the children could play and help out. Bring some laughter. Often also serving as a listening ear. Every night, the only quiet time when both my husband and my mother were at home, having someone else stay with me, they would try to talk for a few minutes. Catch up. Understand what was next and what needed to be done the following day. They tried to keep the routine at home as organized as possible and as similar to what it had been. Everyone was stressed and tired. The girls all got sick, expressing their misery through their bodies.

I was systemically injured. From head to toe. I was hit in my belly and suffered a "belt injury" caused by the belt that protected me. My spleen had to be taken out, my intestines split into many parts, everything mixed up inside. In the emergency operation, the surgeons opened a stoma, a hole in my belly connected to a changeable bag into which all my bowel products would go. This stoma was left open indefinitely. My lungs were full of liquid, imposing stress on my ability to breathe, and had to be drained. Some of my ribs were broken. Also broken were my left foot, ankle, elbow, and left arm, which required additional operations. My left knee was injured, two of the ligaments and the thigh muscle were torn. My tail bone broke, and my back was also mildly injured. This caused pressure on some of the nerves, which created an over-sensation in parts of my left thigh and no sensation in others, lasting for months. I also suffered from severe whiplash, a minor brain injury, acute post-traumatic stress disorder, and more.

Multiple injuries. A shattering of many parts of the physical body. Not a small tremor, quickly letting everything get back into order or place, but rather a big earthquake, inverting the landscape, inviting a full physical re-organization. One that must begin with cleansing the dirt and fallen trees. Then, continue by learning the new topography, as the landscape is not as it was. No back doors left to enter life as it was before. The option of returning to my old body, my old self, was gone.

The physical invitation for re-organization was for the whole of me, inviting me to learn many basic functions. It was an invitation to a new start – a conscious one. I needed to consciously learn how to walk, paying full attention to how I placed my foot. Where do I set it? How do I bring the other one forward? To what angle do I turn my leg, and from where is that turn coming? Is it from my hips? My knee? How do you maintain balance when your core, your abdominal muscles, are gone, torn, or weak? It was learning to physically walk. It was also learning to walk who I am. To walk by a deep truth I was yet to be able to put into words, which simmered within me, following my visit to the luminous fields of pure LOVE. It was learning to walk life itself.

How do I start eating after not eating for weeks? I did not have many intestines left in my body, resulting in a restricted diet. Also, my jaw was injured, and because of my belly injury and the need for what was left of my intestines to heal with the stoma opening, I was receiving nutrients directly into my veins for nearly a month. I was unable to chew. When I was allowed to start eating, I first struggled with opening my mouth wide enough. It felt like my jaws were repeatedly closing on me, and even when I managed, chewing was extremely painful, as it still sometimes is. I still enjoyed it. It felt good to be eating on my own, feeling the different flavors on my dry tongue. Yet, soon after, it was all out on the floor by my hospital bed. In a very gradual process, this required me to eat very consciously. Not in terms of ideology – because something is healthy or not or because of some trend – but from carefully listening to my body. To observe what made my body relaxed, balanced, and comfortable. What does not result in vomiting, bloating, or pain? What helps me control the cyclic activity of my recovering intestines so that I don't feel every point of the joined intestinal sections? What will allow me to control the timing of the output into the bag connected to my body, helping to avoid it happening in public? Later, when all the parts of my intestines recovered and the stoma was closed, I had to learn to operate the whole system from the beginning.

The only way to learn was to be attentive and respectful to my physical body. Doctors and dietitians had their opinions on what was right for me. Much of the advice was very beneficial. Much of it, especially regarding my nutrition, was often not respectful to my observations about myself and my attentiveness to my own body. I was learning that when I listen to my body, it talks, and it can always tell me exactly what it needs.

It was like being a newborn baby. A soul coming into a physical human body. Decreasing its expanded nature into a significantly denser, limited, and dependent form of being. Needing to learn its functions. How does this hand move? What can this body do, and what can it not do? What feels nice and should be repeated, and what should be avoided? I was also literally like a baby: diapers, feeding on "milk" inserted directly into my veins, utterly dependent on others throughout my stay in the hospital and long into my return home.

The choice to embrace re-organization. The choice to heal. To explicitly take responsibility for my recovery process. Being conscious of the alternatives and listening to what was right for me was not easy. My physical state was fragile, with multiple considerations and many doctors involved, each with their perspective on what was right. It constantly invited thought as to what to focus on at each moment. What would most enhance my overall healing, not just the healing of only one of many injuries? Trying to navigate the hospital world, doctors, and medical terms, as well as my dependency, pain, blurriness, and confusion took the little energy I had.

And there was a parallel luminous reality simmering around me – that which I had experienced in my NDE. A reality of beauty, serenity, presence, belonging, acceptance, and LOVE, floating somewhere above me like a white cloud on a sunny day, noticed but unreached. Hovering above me, shading over, allowing a fresher breath. A new knowing that was yet to become conscious, guiding me without my knowledge, delicately trying to weave itself in.

There was one significant motive to reorganize, to choose to heal. My daughters. I yearned to get back home to them. Crawling under the blankets and staying there was not a real possibility. I covered myself more than once. Hiding from everything for a short while, "forgetting" I was more than a patient in the hospital, ignoring the universe calling to me, but it was not an option to stay there. I longed to come home to my daughters; I wished to hug them, play with them, and care for them as I had before. That was the only thing that mattered. I understood that I did not know what I would be returning to, and deep within me, I asked myself how I could be a mother when I was now a baby myself. But I so wanted to. I wanted to be their mother, just as I had unknowingly prayed to be four days before the crash.

Journaling Exercise

Journaling had a significant effect on my healing. Though I did not address it within this chapter, it is the first tool I wish to share with you. My journal was a place to write down my thoughts, confusion, and insights. It began as lists of words, then sentences when I could write more coherently. When in any process of growth or healing, and even when only intending to begin this process, we all benefit from recording our thoughts, feelings, and insights. If you don't already, I invite you to start journaling.

In this exercise, I invite you to journal about the **meaning of parenting** to you.

If you have experience with journaling, open your journal and jump to the questions below. If you are new to journaling, you might wish to make some preparations.

Preparations: Take out a notebook and a pen or pencil that is comfortable for your hand so that your writing can freely spill out. Approach this exercise when you have at least 15 minutes, as it usually takes a few minutes to gather ourselves, center, and put daily events to the side.

If you would like to, light a candle or prepare other ceremonial elements around you (you don't have to, but I find it helps set an intention). Slowing your breath can also help in centering.

Journaling questions: Being a parent / mother / father means:

_____

Write down anything that comes up in fluent sentences or as a list. It's possible that seemingly unrelated ideas will initially come down your pen – write them down as well. Journal until you feel there are no more words asking to come down your pen.

The more you journal, the easier and more fluent it becomes.

Shedding

*M*ANY YEARS AGO, FLOWING *in the river of time, there was a little child. More than anything else in his world, the child loved closing his eyes, feeling his body relaxing into the softness of a white cloud, and going on adventures. Sometimes he would sit on the cloud, his eyes curiously wide open as he swallowed the beauty beneath. Fields and forests, rivers and lakes, mountains and deserts, little villages, distant houses, and big cities. From above, he would see farm animals, cars driving below, and people in their daily work routines. He especially loved watching children play.*

At times he would close his eyes and let the cloud surprise him. On one such day, he woke up where the cloud met a high steep mountain peak. So high that it peeked above the clouds. Its edges were steep, and climbing on it was only for those who knew how. For the first few moments, all the child wanted was for the cloud to back away from the mountain's peak and continue their journey. But no. The cloud reached firmly, stubbornly, toward the mountain. And when the child did not understand that the cloud wanted him to get off onto the mountain's peak and stand on its ground, the cloud slightly shifted its shape, with a laughing smile, into a slide, and the child found himself sliding and standing on the mountain. Both the cloud and the mountain seemed amused. The child was curious.

Then, the mountain spoke. And its voice was so deep that the child's body trembled from the mountain's movement.

"Look around, child," it said with its thundering voice. "Look around in all directions."

The child looked and saw a world. And in each direction he turned, the clouds moved and opened a window for him to see. And the child was touched by the enormous variety of colors, short trees and tall trees, full of leaves or naked of them, endless greens and the blue of the waters, bare ground, and the colors of earth and sand. After looking again and again and again in all directions, swallowing the world around him with his eyes, he sat down on the mountain's topmost rock. For a while, the mountain stayed with the child in his silence. Present. Then, he spoke again, saying "look, child" in his deep thundering voice, spacing his words so that they would not be swallowed by their own echo.

"Look," he said again. "All that you see is both mine and yours. Shared. When you dream me, I become alive, I breathe. My heart, residing deep in my center, knows that you know. And your heart knows that I know. And in this way, even though I am rooted in my place, my hands reaching above, and even though you walk on the earth, gathering, building, and creating, we are always intertwined, one with the other."

The child was quiet, trying to understand what the mountain had just said to him. Many questions were running in his mind. His heart knew that all the mountain said was truth. And even more, that he knew all of it. That it was not new to him. He took a deep breath. He placed his palms on what was next to him, touching the mountain, the rock, the ground, connecting to the mountain, for a moment feeling them being one. Breathing together.

Then, after some moments that felt both as short and long as the shared eternity of their existence, the cloud reached closer to the mountain and called to the child, telling him without any words, "Come. It is time for us to return."

The child looked toward him, wishing to stay with the mountain a little longer. Being himself that is also the mountain. Being the mountain that is also himself. But then, the mountain encouraged him to slide back to the cloud with a tender movement, just as the cloud had done when he arrived.

"I am in your heart," he said to the child. "Always."

The doctors would suddenly come into the room and suddenly leave it. Every few days, the doctors' rounds also included more senior physicians. They would stand crowded around my bed, talking above my head. They would look at the open wound in my abdomen. Ignoring the many other injuries. They spoke fast, and I could not follow any of them. There was only one female doctor, about my age, a mother herself, who always looked me in the eyes, catching my attention. As if saying, "I see you." Seeing me, that is, beyond the wounded, fractured body.

"Why is she still here?" The department head asked one morning, as if I was neither there nor related to the situation.

The physicians discussed sending me home or possibly to a rehabilitation center. I was stunned. How could I go anywhere in this state? Could I be anywhere outside my hospital room, with my abdomen still open? Connected to oxygen? In a wheelchair? Were they not entirely getting the situation? And why weren't they talking about this with me?

Later that day, one of the physicians, a tall, gray-haired man, came by. He compassionately looked into my eyes and said, "I understand."

I was puzzled. He continued, saying that he knew it was hard, but that as much as they liked me, I could not stay there forever, and that it was not because they needed the bed.

He gently pushed the one button still working, saying, "You must return to your girls. Being home, with your family, your things, sleeping in your bed, would be good for you. The best rehabilitation is at home."

We were both quiet. I had no idea what to say. I could have understood if he had said this about someone else. I did not feel it was related to me. After a few silent moments, he explained that, one way or another, returning home was the next step. Though I could try to delay it, it was unavoidable.

It was the first time anyone had talked about this directly with me. I knew they spoke with my husband and mother, and I never wanted to hear anything about it. I was terrified and hung on to my breathing issues, insisting I would not go home dependent on oxygen. After this conversation, they pushed to solve the oxygen dependency. A physiotherapist came in and conducted lymphatic drainage. All of us quietly knowing it was my fear we were working on. Fear of the uncertainty of what was ahead. I was preparing for the next stage of the unknown.

At that stage, the focus was on my physical recovery. I was blurred from the strong painkillers I was still dependent on and had no mental ability to even try to understand what I experienced during those sacred moments immediately after the crash. What was this place I had gone to, which emerged when I closed my eyes? How could I embrace it in my physical presence? I had no idea that what I experienced in the crash had a name, that it is a type of a Near-Death Experience (NDE), and that it is quite a common phenomenon. However, while I was yet to digest what I had experienced and understand what it meant, let alone put it into words, it was all quietly informing every moment of my days. Mainly, it was a hidden internal compass. A deep guiding knowing that, contrary to how things seemed and my vast physical challenges, everything was also precisely okay. It helped me get through one hour, then another, and eventually through each day.

On the drive home from the hospital, I was sitting beside my husband in the new car he had bought. Purple and big. I hated its smell. The almond trees on the mountain slopes close to the hospital shined with their light pink and white flower dresses. I could not breathe. I was astonished. Time in the hospital ran differently, and although I knew that two months had passed, this truth did not permeate my senses. Tears ran down my cheeks while I was gazing from the car window. Tears of fear and excitement. Tears of joy at the sight of the almond dresses and the sadness of realizing how long I had been away from home, from my daughters, from the ones I love most. Tears of ease and a deep knowing that had walked with me since the car crash, my experience of light, together with profound confusion. I dreamed of having a picnic under the trees, dressing in their flowers, and disappearing within them.

I tried to repress the understanding that I had no idea what was ahead. And then, together with being terrified, I also felt a delicate inner, unexpected tingle guiding me, without any doubt, that things were as they should be. It was an illogical, contradictory, clashing inner conflict of fear and complete irrational calm, belief, and trust that had been walking with me since my NDE. How could this whole mess and my broken physical state be what it should be?

My inner constrained beliefs told me that experiencing a car crash, being so severely wounded, and being away from my daughters indicated that something was wrong. Something we never wish would happen to us or others. In parallel, a seed – that began to grow within me during those moments of remembering I am LOVE – reminded me that what I was experiencing, in each tiny moment of reorganizing my body, had a reason. Possibly beyond my ability to ever understand.

Recovering, my mind had no idea what was true anymore. My heart did, but it had yet to carry an organizing mechanism that would explain it, even to itself. I longed for what was just before. The simplicity of the full life of a house with three babies – even the never-ending housework. To be with my family and my daughters. To be a mother to them, to take care of them, to nurse, hug, and play. Fairly little wishes. Enormous in relation to my state. Was that at all possible? By then, it had been two months, which felt like a lifetime, in which others cared for them, and I was absent. Waiting eagerly in the hospital for the short visits of my little ones, and then wishing the visit would end, unable to bear seeing their confusion from the hospital environment and its smells, their mom looking sick and not as they knew her, and my inability to extend even a hand. I was so confused. I was yet to have any words to express what I now know and share: the answers I had returned with to questions I was not aware I had ever asked.

My husband was driving very slowly, fearing causing me any pain. When we entered our village, I wanted to hide, unable to meet any familiar, caring faces. I had clearly requested no welcoming party. He drove slowly through the curves of the hill. We were quiet. Then he turned towards our house. A delicate, slow turn. He constantly looked at me. Both of us knowing that coming back home was more than significant. A moment I had avoided thinking about, and which he had barely dared to dream of. The girls were looking out the window. Waiting. Anticipating. Not knowing what it was they were waiting for, mimicking the anticipation of my parents. The little ones, the twins, not even understanding the meaning of the occasion. On that first night at home, after the excitement waned, and after I showered off all the hospital smells I could, my husband helped me to our bedroom. Our toddler was already lying there, tucked warmly under the blankets, going to sleep. I managed to bring myself to fall on the bed by her side and spontaneously tried to sing her the lullaby we always sang at bedtime. We held hands. I was choking on the words, without breath. We both cried.

Wishes, fantasies, sincere, true intentions, and physical reality. The reality was that I could do none of what I wished for or dreamed of. I was unable to take care of my daughters. I could not feed, cook, bathe, dress, or take care of any of their other needs. I was not nursing anymore; my mix of nurturing milk and blood was dry by then. The wound in my breast was still healing. I could not hold them, even if someone brought them to me, as my left arm was in a cast. My back injury put pressure on some nerves and created a heightened sensitivity to any touch, down to my injured left knee, and my abdomen was still a big open wound. So hugging, playing, or even reading a short children's book were not options. I was able to reach my healthy right hand to touch them a little. I was able to send loving looks with my eyes. There were moments when that was enough for me, for them, or for us both. There were moments when it was not enough, but it was the reality. Clear as a windy rainstorm.

Every little action—those small daily elements of drinking a glass of water, brushing my teeth or hair, getting up, sitting down, changing from one pair of pajamas to another, taking the spoon and loading some food on it, and then directing it to my mouth, that is, after someone else cut the food or mashed it, so that I would need to chew as little as possible—took at least twice as long, if not five times as long, as it would normally. In retrospect, I sometimes wonder whether those sights, the girls seeing their mom like this, affected them. They were very little. Children rarely remember anything from these ages, and my daughters do not hold any conscious memory of those times. Was it just their reality? Children always astonish me in their pure acceptance of things as they are. That is, when we let them. Did they compare me to their grandpa, who, at the time, was dealing with muscular dystrophy and was in a wheelchair and dependent on help? Does it matter in the long run?

In those first few months of recovery, the most basic activities were extremely exhausting, leaving me with no energy for anything other than what I had to do for basic functioning. Energy for being a mom? Energy to do things for my daughters or with them? That was a privilege I had only for short moments, once every couple of days. So, when I was not in the hospital for another checkup, receiving physical therapy or other treatments at home, or getting help with basic functioning, I would rest. Rest in my bed, rest on the couch, rest on an easy chair brought for me from my parents' house. Sometimes in the garden. Between rests, I felt my role was to cooperate, not challenge others by suggesting any changes or even having an opinion. Adding as little as possible extra work for my exhausted family.

It is incredible how it is possible to rest all day, regardless of how active you were before. How, in the flip of a second, one turns from an independent, functioning adult to a dependent one. Beyond the healing injuries, my body was so weak that there was no other alternative. It needed every moment it could rest for its healing. My soul needed those moments of rest to connect within and delicately try to bring to the surface the awakened knowing. A knowing that walked with me from my NDE, trying to reveal itself.

I had the privilege, a necessary one, of others doing everything. Not all parents facing such challenges have the help I had. I needed to care only for myself. And I am forever grateful for it. Days were flying by, a week, and another one. I was slowly able to do a little more, such as sit at the table for longer or stay alert in my resting position on the couch. Watching my daughters cooking food in their play kitchen, or arranging all their dolls and having my father, a university professor, read them all a story. I was still doing only the minimum, focusing on recovering and resting. Or at least trying to. I was doing my best to concentrate on the little moments in which my heart expanded with gratitude, and I felt whole. Or on the moments in which I felt a little bit, a tiny little bit, better. I tried to focus on the slow and gradual progression in my ability to stay stable, take another step, or stay awake for more extended time frames. Some days I was successful. Some days I had no such moments and spent them hiding under my covers, trying to sleep away the pain. The better I got physically, the more my will awakened, tickling me from within. I wanted more, even if I barely had any energy for more than I was doing. It was my heart yearning. Yet, I had no idea what this "more" was about. From time to time, a strong sense would flow through me, a thought and awareness that there was a greater reason I had not died and instead came back. Yet, I had no clear idea what it was. It would flow through me and vanish, and I would return to my rest.

"If you have five good minutes, you can have ten. If you have one good hour, even if the next is a horrible one, it means you can have another good hour at some point and possibly also two," a wise friend told me, at a frustrating moment, with her knowing tone.

"You will see," she continued, "there will be good days!"

I remember looking at her, thinking she did not understand how bad things were. That she just had no idea. It felt like another piece of advice others would recite.

It turned out she knew what she was talking about. Moments slowly accumulated into little chunks, and then I had a good hour here, and another there. Often, at this stage of my recovery, those moments of feeling better were a conscious decision to focus on the good and feeling happy, even if it was fake. A conscious effort, not an authentic feeling. It was intentionally shifting my awareness to what was possible and not to what was lost, never to return.

For a long time, with the way things were, I felt I would never be able to be a mother to my daughters. I was doing nothing of what I had done with them, and for them, before the car crash. My daughters quickly understood that I was not their address for anything. They had enough other adults to turn to. For play, a story, a diaper change, or a cuddle.

Gradually, as time had its way, I internalized that I would probably never be their mother the way I was before. I realized that I had no idea what motherhood truly meant beyond all the daily caretaking activities. That there is a difference between caretaking and parenting, and that the role of a parent is something much deeper and broader than I had ever imagined. What was it? And was there a way for me to be their mother, even if I could not do any of the caretaking? I was yet to embody that all is possible.

A few weeks after my return home, my parents returned to their house. It was mainly about returning to sleep in their house, and maybe having a little time for their own lives. They continued to come to us every day. At that time, my family hired a nanny to be with the twins in the mornings. It allowed my husband to have more working hours and my parents to partially return to their routine. The nanny's presence was confusing for me. Who is in charge? Do I need to be present around them, or is it better that I stay away, rest, and let her be with them? She was doing everything anyway, while I was sitting around. And would her presence interfere with the little bit of connection I was trying to hold onto with MY daughters?

One morning, two friends came along with their babies. Everyone sat on the carpet playing. I sat by them on the couch, blurred in my pain and very uncomfortable. I tried to sit up, chat, and be with them. But the open wound in my abdomen and my weakness were in my way. I could enjoy friends for five minutes at the most. Then I would prefer to be resting. Alone. As much as I wanted to, being social was not a top priority with the little energy I had. Then, seemingly out of the blue, one of the other babies hit one of my twins on her head.

My daughter started crying. I was unable to bend down to reach her or pick her up. For a few short seconds, she looked at

me, puzzled, then transferred her eyes to the nanny standing in the kitchen and the other mothers sitting on the
carpet next to them. I felt trapped. She turned to look at me
again, confused, frozen to her spot, her face wet with tears.
My heart cried. I told my friends, who were also unsure
of the proper reaction, to bring her up to me. We hugged.
I ignored the physical pain. I had to be there for her. It
all happened for merely a few seconds. A significant few
seconds that made me realize that even if I am entirely
unable to do a thing, I am there, I am her mother, and even
if I feel I am unable, they, my daughters, still know me as
their mom and need me.

The nanny was just as confused. She did her best to take care
of my daughters and help in whatever ways she could around
the house. She also tried to respect my presence, stepping away
when I was around, letting my babies' "mother" be with them
when possible. But I was more absent than present. Would it
have been different with another nanny? Maybe. I later met
other mothers in similar situations who had different experiences. Eventually, after a little over three months, we, my
husband and I, asked the one person who loves our daughters
as we do – my mother, their grandmother – to extend herself
even more than she already had, and instead of coming almost
every day in the early afternoon, after picking up our toddler

from her daycare, to also come every morning to be with the twins. They had a present grandmother.

Playing the game of an absent-but-trying-to-be-present parent was overwhelming. On the one hand, there were always other adults, mostly the ones I trusted most: my husband, parents, mother-in-law, and a friend the girls still adore. They all took care of my daughters, loving them, hugging them, and they were fully attentive to my girls' needs. So I could be absent and let go. But then, there were moments when they were not there. Because they went grocery shopping or to pick up our toddler from daycare or took an hour for something in their lives. And there was also my heart that loved my daughters so much, my heart that prayed to "be their mother" and wished to find a way to be present.

Absent-present, present-absent. What does each mean? Where is the unseen border between them? Which active absenteeism can count as resting and healing? Which is an escape? What does it mean to be a present mother? Does sitting quietly on the couch count? Being absent was easier. I yearned for that peaceful state I now knew. I used every opportunity I had to close my eyes and escape into a mode of light.

At that stage of my recovery, it was not intentional. As soon as I closed my eyes, I would either fall asleep or find myself hovering in light, experiencing the memories of my NDE again. It required no effort. It just happened, taking me to places of light where things are just as they are. All made of LOVE, all in the motion of LOVE, full of brightness, clarity, beauty, and calm – a place where my physical challenges did not exist, where my confused emotions softened. A state where I was perfect just as I was. This state made me feel better, physically and emotionally. It would lower the pain level, help me focus and manage the physical therapy exercises, help me relax, and fill me with irrational joy and ease.

It was also an escape from the everyday reality that I was facing. I was responsible only for taking care of myself, which wasn't even possible because I needed help in cutting my food, washing, dressing, getting up, walking, treating my wounds, and replacing the stoma bags. I felt unneeded and, even more, like a burden. My family not only had the three little ones to take care of, but they also needed to take care of me. They were grateful to have me with them. It was I who felt I was adding to the load. So while my will and longing to become my daughters' mother was pushing me forward, it was also pushing me away, as I felt I could do nothing about it.

I found myself living in Dreamtime. Like a large old cottonwood tree in a snowy winter. Going into a long, distant hibernation. All my leaves falling off, my bark wrinkled. Having those who pass by me, maybe gracefully touching my skin, wonder if I will wake up again when spring comes. I was not clearly dead. I was not alive, either.

I needed to acknowledge and look into the eyes of all that had changed. I have an optimistic nature, and facing all that was lost was unbearable for me. Like on a hike, when you must go on and acting cheerful makes you feel better, I found myself smiling at everyone and being positive, playing "being happy." Barely acknowledging that I was crying within. I was disheartened by the dreams I had carried just before. Unwilling to accept that, most likely, we would not have more children as we had planned to, when I should have been grateful for the three beautiful ones we had. I could not swallow all the changes in so many layers of my being at once. I was miserable about how I looked and the body I no longer knew, devastated by the distance from my daughters, drained from the inevitable game of being more absent than present, and helpless at the sight of my husband's exhaustion, trying to manage to be a full-time parent and a full-time caregiver to me, while working and more.

I could not bear the routine everyone tried to keep as it was before. Some of our previous habits did not seem fitting anymore. It was an inner feeling and not a sense I could communicate. Overwhelmed, I tried to stay away from others when I could, trying to avoid visits from friends and family. It was me avoiding social events, and it was me who was unhappy when I missed them, even if it was just an hour at the park with friends to allow me some quiet resting time. I was also miserable when my family missed them because of me, but I was sad when they went, leaving me behind. Confused like a tree, about to let its first spring leaves bud, then having a spring snowstorm, and then another, and another, freeze the world around it back to the stillness of the white.

I was angry about being unable to do so many basic things. Angry at those who had time with my daughters, knew them, spent time with them, and were there for them instead of me. I was angry with the doctors for some small mistakes they made during my hospital stay. I focused on all the things they disregarded as crucial, but which affected my quality of living, instead of on the fact that they prioritized saving my life and did an amazing job. I was angry with myself for not managing to be more present for my girls. I felt some elements of our lives should be handled differently, but I was not able to communicate it to my family. When the frustration and anger would overwhelm me, I would distance myself from others. These were not familiar feelings, and I did not know how to deal with them. With the huge load all the others were carrying, I did not feel I had any right to anger, confusion, opinions, or the like.

Something within my perception of life shifted. I looked at small events around me – words said, games played, ordinary daily things – and I felt that some of them could be lived differently. The seed that woke up in my NDE and the perspective I unconsciously acquired while overlooking the shimmering white balcony were starting to change my everyday perceptions, words, and thoughts. It was a new understanding of who we are as humans, where we come from, and our ways here. It was not a new truth. It was new to me. Answers to questions I never consciously asked, slowly bringing themselves into my awareness. However, I was still processing it all myself and was still unable to express it. The gap between what I felt was my truth and my ability to express it confused and discouraged me. I was like a caterpillar, already in its cocoon, still undergoing transformation. Not a caterpillar anymore. Not yet a butterfly. But already feeling the inner call to emerge. It felt as if the world I left on the day of the car crash was unlike the one I came back to. I had crossed a sea. I had no way to return to what was.

It was not the world that had changed. It was I who had experienced something significant and returned with a new pair of lenses. I had no idea what I thought of the world anymore, trying to behave as if everything was the same, while within, things felt different. I worked hard to fit in and be as I was before. Not that it was realistic with my multiple injuries, nor was it good for me, but at that stage of my healing journey, I still tried. I tried to join in the pickups from daycare because my daughter wanted me to pick her up as I used to and as the other mothers did. I tried to go out with them to a picnic or to visit their other grandpa. The little ones did not understand why I was staying behind. My surroundings wanted me to return to who I had been. To be doing more and more of what I would have been doing if the car crash had not occurred. For them, any sign of return meant I was healing. I was coming back to myself. To who I was, to who they loved and knew. For me, it meant I was again deviating from my path, driving on a dead-end road.

The car crash created a complete displacement of my physical body, inviting a new physical beginning, like a newborn, together with an awakened ability to visit realms of light and LOVE, and to remember our source – LOVE. It did not contradict the belief system I had carried before. It actually met some spark of knowing within me that had waited quietly to ignite. Yet, it was not a conscious system of thought or beliefs. Consequently, having no framework to understand what I was experiencing was another source of challenge and frustration. I had gotten a new beginning but had no idea how to embrace it and integrate it into my life and my family's lives. The rug had been pulled from under my feet and replaced with an invisible one I had yet to understand. It was there, but I could not use it as a base for understanding. I felt I was walking on empty air. I did not talk about it, and not talking about it made me sometimes question myself. Question something that lived powerfully and intensely within me, like nothing ever had before.

In my first attempts to share my experience, I carefully picked people who I thought might relate and possibly provide a guiding perspective. But I could not find the words. They would look at me very puzzled and shift the conversation elsewhere. Sharing openly, as I do here now, took me a long time. Years. I needed to first heal in all layers of my being. I needed to find the words to express something that words cannot communicate and bridge the gap between the two realities I felt I was living in. Slowly learning to see the beautiful colors of my new invisible rug.

Time has its way. The water flowing in the river continues carving its way through the earth and stone, knowing which cracks it should rush into and widen and which to avoid. From month to month, I was getting better. The cast on my left arm was taken off. My intestines healed well, and I was operated on to have the stoma closed. I was more stable and walking better. My nutrition improved, and I kept learning what is respectful of my body and what is not. I stopped losing weight and looked a little more human, and physical therapy was making me stronger.

A little over a year after the car crash, my husband and mother looked for a car I would be comfortable driving. The one they found was available only in black. I agreed to try it if we find a way to change its color. I needed happiness. So we found colorful hippie bumper stickers and covered the car with flowers, butterflies, bees, and more. It made me happy. I think it also made the drivers who saw our car, when it was not dusty, smile too. It made me feel a little safer. I started practicing driving again, first just around the block with someone by my side. Then, slowly, I started driving on my own, which helped me become a bit more independent. This is crucial when living in a small village with no public transportation. I was now able to drive to my appointments at the rehabilitation center. I was very proud of myself every time I managed to get there and whenever I parked back at our house. The girls would hear the car pulling into the driveway and often stand and look out the window. Waiting. Reminding me of those moments of my return home from the hospital. After parking, I always had to take a few moments to breathe. To relax. To get back to my core. Only then could I carefully pull myself out of the car, grab my walking stick, get stable, and sigh with relief.

About two months after I started driving again, I accepted an invitation to return to teaching an academic course. Before the car crash, I was about to begin a part-time position in the psychology department of a college close to where we lived. At that time, just after giving birth to the twins, I was teaching some BA and MA classes and decided that I did not wish to go for a full-time, tenure-track position. A part-time position felt like something I could manage more easily as a young mother. The car crash changed all my plans.

When the college invited me to return to teach just one class, I felt it could help me get back into life. Teaching was something I had always enjoyed. I also did not want to lose that job opportunity, which seemed, at the time, to be one I could manage in parallel to my continued rehabilitation and recovery. It was close to where we lived, and my colleagues there were all extremely friendly and helpful. At first, I taught just two hours a week. Then, the next semester, I tried to teach two sections of the same course. I was horrible! My abilities were not as they were before the crash. My brain became sluggish. If, before the car crash, I was considered an excellent teacher, I now did not remember what was on the next slide, what I had to say, or what a student had just asked. I was creative in compensating, but it took enormous effort, which was unfair to my students and me.

I sat for hours trying to prepare the course material in ways that would help me teach it properly. Course material I had been fluent in before. I experienced the absurdity of how being "cured" is often measured only by your function in the work environment. Can you work? Do you work? How much can you work? And if you can, even if you are not doing a good job, or if it is damaging your health, then you may check the box and announce you are cured. I was trying hard, wasting all my energy on those classes instead of on my healing and time with my family. Not realizing that social conventions, such as seeing work as a criteria for being a functional adult, or having to be active and successful, were taking over me again. I was putting aside that inner pulse asking me to listen, trying to remind me who I was, to remember what I had been through, trying to show me other ways of thinking, feeling, and participating in the world together with all my physical challenges. According to social standards, I was getting better. Inside, I was dying. Again.

I could no longer do any of the things I used to define myself by, though I still tried to define myself by them. The faculty needed me to return for more teaching hours, resume conducting research, and continue publishing academic papers. I could not even do the little teaching I was doing. I had to stop teaching. I had to give up on this academic position. Or any academic future, for that matter. I was petrified – and relieved. I could not take the frustration for one more minute. I felt like I had been thrown into a vast, hollow space. Not a teacher. Not able to go back to doing research or anything I had been doing before, avoiding social events and people. I no longer looked as I used to. I was skinny and looked weak and unhealthy.

Every day, every week, I realized that another layer of who I thought I had been was no longer relevant. I was shedding my skin, again and again, becoming stripped of so many defining characteristics I had carried with me for years. I was like an onion, peeling layer after layer, trying to find that sweet center, to discover there is more to peel on the way. Shedding more and more characteristics of myself, sometimes ones I did not know existed. I felt empty, unneeded, and lost. Being a parent to my daughters was the only defining role in my life that still mattered. The one I was not willing to give up on. But it also needed shedding so that I could see other parenting paths. Find the parenting within me, and not the one playing by what social expectations and archetypes define. I felt there must be another way, a way I had yet to discover, to be present and be their mother along with all my limitations and challenges. My heart yearned for answers. I could not bear the possibility that the situation would remain as it was.

The shedding and emptiness, confusing and heavy, was freeing up space. Once freed, it slowly enabled the LOVE hovering over me to weave through its delicate golden thread, shifting my attention to my heart and towards questions of being. The two separate realms I was experiencing began to slightly merge. I learned that as long as I focused on the physical acts I performed as a mother – or rather, did not perform – there would be no room for any new learning to take place; there would be no further understanding to merge with my inner core. This does not mean that doing is insignificant. But I gradually began to understand that there was an element of parenting inviting me to explore it. An element that stretches far beyond tending to one's children, crucial and loving as that tending may be. An essential aspect of parenting that goes beyond the doing or not-doing, still outside my awareness or reach, but already slightly visible on the far horizon.

I was heartbroken by acknowledging that my love for my daughters was previously manifested mainly through actions. That it was very unlike the LOVE that surrounded me in my NDE and that I felt around me as soon as I would close my eyes, hovering again in the luminous fields of my memories. I desperately wanted to share this pure LOVE, unconditional and expanding, with my daughters and family: to love them and to have them know they are loved in that whole, unquestioned, tranquil, accepting, and soft way. Much later, when I started sharing the story of my NDE with others, some reflected that to their understanding, we are not supposed to live LOVE here on Earth as we experience it in NDEs and similar events. That it is not meant to be the same in the first place. Nevertheless, while observing this gap between realities myself, something in me kept pushing, unconsciously knowing it is possible to live this LOVE here, within our dense bodies, and that all of us and all of our children can walk it within their lives. Everything that was transpiring questioned all that I previously knew.

I was searching for meaning – a meaning that would characterize me as the mother of my daughters. That would be the sprouting of a new onion, not the peeling of it. A significant, meaningful nature that would emerge beyond all the actions performed by other family members. The profound and vital role of a mother, of being the mother that I wished to be, seemed farfetched and unrealistic in the context of what was happening at the time of my absence. I sought to impart to my children LOVE in its essence. I desired to understand its meaning and learn how to utilize it for a parent-child relationship. Deep within me, I knew it was possible. But how?

Letting Go – Releasing What Does Not Serve Us

Any belief system and all defining roles are limiting, including that of being a parent. A crucial part of any healing journey is shedding what limits us, but shedding limiting beliefs about parenting does not mean we stop being parents. It is about taking ourselves a step closer to the essence of parenting within us. Allowing the dead leaves to fall. Cleansing elements, definitions, and expectations that are not ours or that were ours but no longer serve us.

Healing often starts with awareness. Like the dust accumulating on a shelf. If we don't see it, we won't clean it. Sometimes, as soon as we are aware, all we need to do is blow on the dust slightly, and it's gone.

Mind maps are my preferred tool for growing awareness. While mind maps can be used for many purposes, when used to spark our awareness, we freely jot down whatever comes up.

Preparations: Prepare your journal or blank paper and some colorful pens or pencils. If you would like to, light a candle, or prepare other ceremonial elements around you.

Steps:

1. At the center of your page, draw a circle (or any other shape). In the circle, write the question – "What am I ready to shed?"

2. From the circle, draw a few lines, like a sun, leading to empty circles.

3. Take a deep breath, trust your heart, and write whatever comes up in those empty circles. Some limiting beliefs, behaviors, or habits will be straightforward, and other ideas may seem irrelevant at first. Leave your judgment aside, and write it all down.

4. Write different elements or ideas in different circles, shapes, and colors.

5. Sometimes, after we write an idea down, more related thoughts come up. Pull out additional lines, add new circles, squares, or triangles, and create another smaller sun.

6. When done, take a deep breath. Look at everything that you wrote. Ask yourself, "What am I ready to release and shed? Are there any additional habits? Actions? Forgiveness? Lifestyle changes? Self-acceptance? Other elements?"

7. Some people finish in one sitting. Others may wish to work on their mind map of releasing and shedding for a few

days, allowing the intention of release to awaken and bring forward additional elements. I suggest taking no more than three days. You can always start another one and deepen your process.

A Releasing Fire

Fire has a transformative quality. You can take the mind map you created with everything you wrote and burn it carefully in a small fire. Give it to the fire with the intention and prayer that any energy no longer serving you, which can easily be released, be released by the fire.

Make it a ceremony. Acknowledge with gratitude the many gifts brought by the lessons and learnings from all that you no longer need.

Some of what you wrote will be released, and some may need deeper resolutions. You can continuously bring awareness using additional mind maps with the same intention or use other modalities to spark your awareness of what needs releasing and have as many such releasing fire ceremonies as you feel called to.

Always thank the fire and Spirit, God, Tao, or The One, as you relate to it.

Going Inward

MANY YEARS AGO, FLOWING in the river of time, there was a human. He was tall and fairly skinny. His long hair and long beard were turning gray. On his back, he carried a faded blue backpack. His facial expression was dull and vague. He was walking. He was walking through a field of grain. His gaze was always forward. Never down at his feet. Never to his sides, or up to the blue sky above. Forward. Directly to the far horizon before his eyes.

On the day of our story, he was walking until dusk, when the setting sun dazzled him, and he had no choice but to stop for a moment. He stood there in the middle of the grain field. Grain. Growing, green, fresh, all around. For the first time in his long life, he diverted his gaze down. Uncomfortably noticing that he was walking in the same place. And that under his feet, the green, fresh grains were all crushed.

He lowered his head, saddened. All he could ask himself was, "how can I get out of here?" He looked for the field's nearest edge, thinking he would make his most gigantic leaps. Thinking he would try to step on the stems of the growing green grain as little as possible. And so he leaped, and leaped, and leaped, but the field of growing, fresh grain stayed just as large. The leaps did not take him any closer to the edge of the field, to clear ground.

The human stood still, crying for help, not knowing what to do next. His legs started to shake slightly, deepening their hold within the earth below. He felt his legs pulled down into the ground. Deep, deep down. The earth was warm, inviting, smelling fresh and new, and it opened and gently guided him within until he found himself standing in a big, beautiful cave. And in the cave, there was a stream of pure water. And on the other side of the stream, children were playing.

"What are you doing here?" The children looked at him and asked.

He did not know the answer to their question, so he shared his story. His story of walking. His story of walking in the fields of grain, green, growing, and fresh. His story of finding that he had been walking in the same place and trying to find his way out without crushing any more stems. Leaping, leaping, leaping. His story of the earth, warm and inviting, opening and guiding him in. Into this beautiful cave.

The children wondered about the aim of his visit. Then, a small child, young in his years, came quietly forward and said: "For me, you came."

The human and the child looked one into the eyes of the other, drowning in the pure reflection of the stream until they became one.

"Truly. For you, I came. And I did not even know you were lost."

"It is my time to go now," said the child, hugging all his friends. Then he jumped over the stream, directly into the human's heart. The human, surprised, found he expanded. His heart widened. He hugged the small child who had just jumped in.

An opening emerged at one end of the cave, and light came in from afar. The human waved goodbye to the playing children, expressing his gratitude for their hospitality, and walked through a tunnel in the cave towards the light. He climbed some rocks, then descended again until he reached the cave's opening.

The child said to him, "You must protect me. I have not seen the light of the sun for many long years."

The human asked, "How come? You are made of radiant, glowing, shiny light."

"I have been hiding," said the child. "I have been hiding from the voice of a shout, from insecurity and lack of trust. I have been hiding from ignorance and the destructive power of words. I have been hiding from the uncertainty of knowing whether we will have a piece of bread for breakfast or not. I have been hiding from our mother's illness, from our father's hard days."

The human was silent for a moment.

"You are safe now," he promised. He covered them both with a scarf of love and took a few steps outside into a shaded area.

"Would you like to look around?" The human asked the child within him. The child opened his eyes and glanced outside. His heart expanded from the beauty of the world: flowers and green, birds and butterflies, prosperity and abundance, giving, sharing, and a reaching hand. Purity and innocence. His heart was whole. Their heart was whole.

Flowing in the river of time, there is a human. He is tall and fairly skinny. His long hair and long beard, turning gray. On his back, he carries a faded blue backpack. A smile on his face. The man is walking. Slowly walking. Not minding that he does not know where. He makes sure not to harm any stems of grain or others on his way. To stop where he can reach out a hand. Sometimes he sleeps under the branches of an old tree, hearing the tree's stories through his heart. Sometimes he stops in a village and joins its people in their work. And when he is not sure of the way, when he finds himself at a crossroad, he stops, he takes some deep breaths, he sits as long as it takes, reaching his roots deep into the earth, and his branches up into the sky, and then he asks the child of light, who is him himself, who returned to him within the cave, where to turn now. Sometimes this new road is paved, abundant with fruit growing by its sides, and good clear water flows in the streams along its sides. Sometimes, it is a steep path, inviting a climb on a high mountain. He is grateful for the paved one. He is grateful for the steep one. He is walking his path. And evermore, he is not walking it alone. He himself, his essence, his light, is walking with him. Together, they always know the way.

What did I lose in my years here on Earth, and when? And what do I need to find within me, or in a secret cave, to become my daughters' mother again? To expand? To walk with peace, being my essence, like the human in the story? Can we feel the divine LOVE I felt during my NDE here on Earth, grounded in its soil, within our dense bodies? How can I share what

I experienced with my daughters as more than their mom's story? Have them live it as their everyday reality? Avoid stepping in that same spot of crushed grains? How do I share with them the profound feeling of acceptance, nonjudgement, tranquility, and guidance that I felt in my NDE? Is it possible to feel this beauty, light, and LOVE in our here and now?

I was overwhelmed with questions. In one moment, I was sitting on the living room's purple couch with an open heart, hope sparkling in my eyes. And in another, I was on the same purple couch, disconnected, my eyes half-closed, my body bending over, unintentionally jumping at any noise or sudden movement made around me. As if I was not there at all. I, too, had been walking in the same spot for years, unknowingly crushing fresh green stems of grain, making huge leaps in the same place. Thinking to myself, "oh, how wonderful this green meadow looks," and "so much color, so many interesting things and opportunities," continuing from college to my master's degree and then a Ph.D. Starting to realize I was in the wrong meadow only when I reached my post-doctoral studies. It was not my true path, and deep within me, I had always known.

Since my childhood, from time to time, I would sense an invitation to explore more than I was, an inner call to see not only through my physical eyes. To open up to more of the possible and the ever-greater richness of our world. For each step I took towards these invitations – agreeing to see using my inner eyes, being directed, or knowing something deeper about a coming situation – I took several steps back. I ignored the messages. Was terrified when the guidance I received came true. This intuitive knowing and feeling about myself and others always seemed so far from the rational, academic environment I grew up in. It scared me. It was not something I could rationally understand or explain. I was unaware of those I could have possibly consulted or told what I was experiencing. So I developed mechanisms that helped me avoid these little invites. Which meant I was ignoring a core piece of my essence.

At home, recovering on our purple couch, my mind was still controlled by the analytic mechanisms it knew. The fewer painkillers I needed, the more my mind clarified, and I could think again. Between moments of hope and sparkling eyes to moments of disappearing and dozing off, I found myself lying on our couch, observing my daughters' needs, and trying to analyze whether I could meet any of them at that time. Desperately wishing to find my way back to them. What were the odds? What was affecting the various chances I had? If x or y happened, would things progress faster? And to what extent? Would my recovery correspond to their growth? Children grow so fast.

Mostly, I would doze off at the beginning of this stream of statistical calculations. I had yet to realize that I was no longer standing in the middle of a grain field, unable to get out without stepping on my stems. Nor that my inner flame was burning and lighting my way. I contemplated the various aspects, full of questions about what is right and how to approach my daughters. Tightly holding to what I knew before. I allowed my mind to take control. Playing a "what if" game.

When not in my mind, I turned to other sources of information. Especially books. Miraculously, books on NDEs found their way to me. Before my experience, I had not read any NDE stories or books on the subject. Now, more and more books showed up, and I started to actively look on the web for stories of others' experiences. They all confirmed that what I had experienced was not of my imagination and was a widespread phenomenon. It had a name! And so many shared characteristics. This information nourished the new understandings I had come back with, delicately empowering the truth that had bubbled within my cells since my NDE.

I wondered why I had not experienced the tunnel that kept returning in many NDE stories. Then, I found reports that since everything happens so fast in car crashes, other people who experienced NDEs did not have a memory of the tunnel either. I was a little relieved to find that there are also individual aspects we each experience beyond the common characteristics. It made sense that these correspond with the event that prompted our NDE, the reason for the NDE, and the teachings it invited into our lives.

I also searched for books on parenting in situations like mine. I wanted stories of being absent, trying to heal, and maybe even stories of parents who experienced an NDE and how it affected their parenting. Unfortunately, none of what I found related to parenting – the one aspect I was desperately in need of understanding more about.

Few parenting books I found at the time met me directly in my heart. Quite a few were more confusing than helpful. The spiritual aspect was missing, and although the advice they shared made sense, something within me felt they were not necessarily corresponding with the steps I needed to take or the parenting guidance I looked for. Similarly, this book, my story, and the ideas I am slowly sharing here may be the exact guidance you need or may meet you in an understanding that your path requires different guidance. I find it beautiful that we have so many modalities and routes to healing and parenting.

I also tried to consult others. However, there were always at least two different approaches for every question we had. For example, before my stoma was closed, I wondered what my daughters should know, especially our toddler, since there was the potential that I would have it my whole life. One psychologist told us our daughters should know nothing at this stage and that we should completely hide it. A stoma nurse who guided me on how to clean it, change the bags, and introduced various soothing products, said my daughters should see everything, even the physical opening of the skin that revealed my intestines. She added that it is better to show them intentionally, not have them see it unintentionally and get frightened. Another psychologist said we should treat it naturally and see what happens; it is part of me now. That was a most confusing suggestion. How can one naturally relate to an opening of the intestines on the abdominal skin? With time, once it indeed becomes part of you and the routine of life, I could clearly see how I could, but at the beginning, when still adjusting to things myself?

The thing about deep personal quests is that you cannot search for the answers. The answers find you while you are on your journey, in their intended timing. Others can guide us. Books may resonate, propose a direction, or awaken questions. The answers. My answers. Your answers. The deep and real ones must be figured out by each of us. For me to own what I learned and embrace the gifts of this journey, I had to go through it myself. Heal what requested healing and own everything this journey brought as my power and understanding. Claim its teachings and have it become part of my family's actual life.

It was a dance. One step forward. Two steps back. Contacting, releasing, turning. Physical movement. Standing still. Holding the position. Isolating. Only one body part moving. And once more. And again. And again. A dance between the physical reality, the outer world, and that of the inner movement simmering within me. A flow taking place in the stillness. Needing a clear stage for it to be truly safe to extend the dance. Fly. Embrace the music. Letting it be the one who leads. The tear-inducing, rotting onion in me stood in the center, limiting any flowing movement, continuing to peel its layers.

I was shedding so many personal and professional self-definitions, trying to learn, unfortunately, with only very partial success, to accept the loving care provided to my daughters by others. Slowly grasping that the care I am able or unable to provide is not what defines our relationships. Not that I knew at the time what did. I tried to learn to accept the enormous confusion I was walking in and that it was part of the journey. That what would calm the confusion was not solutions but stillness. The kind of stillness and connectedness I experienced in my NDE. I tried to peel away the many times I fell into those low moments of sadness, anger, or frustration. I had to accept the inherent uncertainty that came to our lives – living as if there is no tomorrow, as the car crash had upturned any certainty we had in life – and also to realize that for some life moves, such as buying a house that could better fit my limitations, a look into the near future may also be reasonable.

Mostly, when I would embrace the music, letting it lead the dance, I would drift into the light, traveling to healing realms. To LOVE. It was the one thing that always felt good. At first, I had only found myself there unintentionally as soon as I would close my eyes. Now, however, I was often able to intentionally take myself there, to other realms. To float in the healing lights of the universe. I also learned that I could go to these healing dimensions when undergoing medical examinations or treatments and desensitize myself. Close my eyes, get there by imagining it, jumping directly to those safe places of my NDE memory, and avoid feeling the anxiety and stress of the treatment. It would always lower the pain level. The doctors would sometimes be surprised, not all of them liked it, yet most never wanted to know where I went or how it helped. "Drifting" to dimensions of LOVE and light became a daily intentional journey. On days when I felt weak and rested more, I would let go and fly with my inner music more than once – slowly embracing it as a more natural part of my daily being. I needed the resting time to connect.

During these explorations, a door opened for me to finally listen within, to myself, to who I was, and to my heart's yearning. I started a journal. A journal for personal writing. An outlet for my thoughts, feeling, and challenges. From time to time, especially if I was tired, I would unintentionally shift from personal writing to automatic writing, sometimes referred to as soul or free writing. Comforting and companionate words would come down my pen. I did not know what the source was. Was it my higher self? Guidance? At the time, it did not matter, as it was always warm. Always loving. Always at the high frequency of existence I felt when traveling back to the dimension of light. I had no reason not to trust it.

Going inward through personal writing, soul writing, and intentional journeying meant connecting to who I was. It was not about knowing the details of my destiny or what I should be doing once I got stronger and my wounds healed. It was a delicate sense of expansion and a change of frequency. Embodying the openness and the possible within me. Owning the realization, walking with me since my NDE, that I am more than a physical – and in my case, fractured – body. That there is much more to my existence than what I can name in my literal, concrete life.

The more these understandings bubbled within me, the harder it became to continue playing the game around me. The game I had constructed and invested in for many years. A game that was pushing me to heal fast, to become the promising woman I no longer was. The game of the academic environment, having to excel, know everything, be smart. A competitive game of inner perfection. A game lead by the mind and the ego, not by the heart. I was recovering from the car crash, reorganizing my body, and my soul wanted to say its words as well. Going back to what had been, the type of work I had been doing, my full-day schedules, and the fast life was not what it was calling for, and it was telling me that through my body.

My heart was drumming one thing within me, while so many other loud noises played their own music all around. Just as they had played before. I felt as if my mind and being were spinning. At times, I wondered which part of what I was sensing was my truth, which resulted from my active imagination, and which came from the music of those around.

Connecting to myself was empowering. Connecting to myself was also very scary. The wholeness and the fears came together, just as when it had been time for me to leave the hospital. I was partially living in other dimensions. Dependent on my journeys to them to feel calm and better in my daily physical routines. I was afraid to lose contact with physical reality. Others around me were definitely thinking, sometimes aloud, that I was losing my mind. That what I was starting to share was the fruit of my active imagination. Questioning my experience. Still, as frightening as the confusion was, something within me kept pushing me to return, explore, and go back. Like a strong unseen magnet. It was more than an escape from the challenging reality of physical limitation, the shedding of everything I thought I knew about myself, and the absent parenting; it was a strong force within, one related to who I am, to deep ancient knowledge. It was stronger than my fears.

I took a friend's suggestion to try energy healing. It was not something I had experienced before, and with my limited perceptions carried from before the car crash, I did not believe in its power. But it was a powerful experience. The healing of physical and emotional limitations through the clearing of energetic heritage, trauma, and more. It spoke the same language as the frequencies of my NDE and significantly pushed me forward in my healing journey. I wanted to know more.

Shortly after I started to work with the energy healer, I gathered the abilities I did not have and challenged myself to a three-day introductory energy workshop that required traveling daily to a big city about an hour away. City roads terrified me, with so many cars around. They still do. Using public transportation would have taken much longer. My thoughts were going wild about it: "What if I can't get a place to sit on the bus? I can't hold myself stable standing. But then, if I drive, what if I can't find close parking? And what if someone honks, and I stress and lose my focus, and what if..." "Breathe," my husband repeatedly told me, and eventually, as he suggested in the first place, I agreed that he would drive me there.

The journey with the energy healer and the experience of an energy healing workshop, basic as it was, were the final confirmations I needed to embrace the energetic reality that I had been sensing since I came back from the NDE. Although everything I was experiencing was so powerful and beyond any fears, I needed these experiences of meeting others pulled to that same world, seen beyond our five senses, to allow myself to surrender to its calling within me. To the invitations I had been feeling all along. It was a jump back in, back to my inner pulse. Back to the knowing I had come back with from the NDE. I slowly built my trust and confidence in the truth bubbling within me. It was hard not to, as it resonated so strongly with everything in my journey. All the pieces started falling into place, confirming that it was indeed my truth.

In time, I got some books on shamanism and learned that what I was doing was similar to shamanic journeying. Simplified, shamanic journeying can be viewed as a form of meditation. In a way, one can refer to it as advanced guided imagination, in which some sections of the guidance are left open and elements that we cannot make up ourselves can be experienced.

It is a basic tool in shamanic practices and is also used in many other spiritual modalities. When journeying, we intentionally expand our awareness, our dream body, our luminous body (we give it various names) and travel to other dimensions, allowing ourselves to experience and see what cannot be seen through our physical eyes. One can travel to different dimensions of reality, experience energetic aspects of our physical reality, communicate with guidance, retrieve information, mediate healing, and more. The mythical healing stories shared at the beginning of each chapter in this book come to me, in the form of simple shamanic journeying, as images that evolve into stories.

At the time, I was traveling to one specific destination: the beautiful, calm, quiet, tranquil space I found myself visiting during my NDE. Some journeys would just calm me down, infuse me with the brightest, purest LOVE ever. In some, I found vivid memories of what I saw from that shimmering white balcony and the teachings they brought. Sometimes, I would find myself seeing reflections of myself, very slowly finding more about why I experienced the car crash and the NDE and why I was going back there, again and again.

I did try other forms of relaxation techniques, various breathing exercises, mindfulness, and meditations. However, as with any modality, some work for some and others for others. One must find what works for them. When I tried to sit to meditate and free my thoughts, my whole body screamed in pain. When I tried meditating lying down, noticing my thoughts and then letting them stream away, trying to clear my mind, I would fall asleep. I tried. So many people told me that meditation would help, but my lack of success was naturally just adding to my frustration instead of reducing it. For some time, I found myself working with sound and movement as much as my challenged body allowed. Finding creative ways to quiet my unsettled mind and open access to my heart. What I did not know at the time was that what I was doing, this drifting into the light, is also an accepted form of meditation. Just not the one everyone is familiar with. Its results were the ones I was looking for, and more.

Using shamanic journeying as an active form of meditation and writing while doing so not only helped me focus and avoid being distracted or falling asleep – it was another step inward. It was not yet any learning at the layer of the mind, but a repeated exposure to what's beyond. Re-experiencing myself there – accepted, loved, perfect as I am. Re-experiencing the light that surrounds us. A repeated confirmation that strengthened the flame now burning within me. It was a knowing of our essence, which we all have the potential to sense when we agree to listen to it. An inner knowing that runs within our cells and our hearts. Not the knowing of the mind. I was listening within and connecting to the LOVE that bubbled within me. And from this bubbling essence of LOVE, I gained more and more inner understanding of who we all are and of our journeys. Remembering something we all know deep down in the center of our existence.

This journey inward confirmed to me again that, as I experienced in my NDE, I was indeed more than my physical body. That we all are. It connected to the compassionate and creative aspects of my soul and who I was in my essence. Beyond the specific clothing I am wearing for this lifetime, such as my red hair, spectacles, or countless freckles. This clarity of being more than a body, the reorganization of my physical form together with the integration of the NDE, led to growing clarity not only in my inner world but also in my outward life. Starting to touch on who I was as an essence connected the dots. I was calmer. What was right for me related to physical elements, such as nutrition, had to align with what I felt as something greater. Accepting myself as more than my physical body meant accepting others as more as well. Realizing I know only a little about the ones I love most. What I learned about myself and about what was right for me bubbled into my physical reality. And from my reality, it bubbled to those around me, to my daughters, and eventually to the writing of this book.

I was choosing health. Health in all layers of my being. In terms of my physical state, and in line with what social norms label as health, my cup was still half full and half empty. It was a choice to focus on the full part. It was the focus. I wanted to heal, not just cure my wounds. I wanted to discover in what ways I could be a mother to my daughters, not focus on the ways I was absent. It was a choice. I could not choose that unclear empty part of the cup. I had to find out what was in the fullness. It was a choice built by many small moments of clarity until it suddenly became the way itself. This aware and conscious choice was driven from places so deep within me that I had no idea they existed. Pushing me to heal. I was inspired by the calm knowing that had walked with me since the car crash, enforcing itself repeatedly when I journeyed or journalled. Supported by the new physical reorganization of my body and by shedding almost all the definitions I had collected through this life, freeing lots of space. I was not changing. I was emerging from a cocoon. A cocoon I had not known existed.

I was remembering me. Like the human who found a part of himself he never knew he lost, deep in the Earth's cave. I was remembering what makes me happy, what makes my eyes sparkle in their depths, what makes my heart beat with joy. It was all little things. My daughters creating a mud pool in the garden and swimming in it. The perfection of fruit. The taste of fresh food. Being out in nature as much as possible. A good talk with a close friend. Reading, reading, and reading. Crafts. Especially sewing, which for me is like meditation. I was remembering what awakens my gratitude. The kind nature of people, the flowers growing, the trees in all their seasonal configurations. Laughing. Being stupid. Toys. The stars at night, the sunset just before. Having a bonfire. Staring into it.

The more definitions and layers I shed, the more I could see me. Recognize me and remember me. Those moments of remembering were moments of grace. Moments of feeling whole. They were moments of being. Being me. These moments of remembrance brought the gift of insight. I noticed that when they took place, my feelings were reaching closer and closer to the feeling of LOVE I knew from my NDE: unconditional, weightless, embracing, and peaceful. These moments of being me were being LOVE. Letting the energy, the essence we are made of shimmer into my being, reminding me again and again who I am. It was feeling it all without journeying to other dimensions of reality, not during a car crash and an NDE. It was being whole. One with the universe. One with all. Here on Earth. In my dense physical body. In awareness. During casual days.

Being one with the universe was heart-expanding but sometimes also too much, inviting me to search for harmony. One
morning, we woke up to a loud noise in the yard. I felt an
unexplained pain all over my body. We went out to find our
landlord at the time, a big-hearted man, a man of the earth, an
aged farmer, driving with his blue tractor, forwards and backward, crashing into an old, ill palm tree, with the intention of
making it fall. His purpose was to help the tree finish its life.
It was very ill. For me, each driving forward, each crash into
the tree felt like I was being crushed into myself. I felt a sudden
pain, running from my toes to my head. I felt the tree's pain in
every cell of my body. We were both unrooted and displaced. I
froze. I could do nothing to help but burst into tears.

After many such episodes, an empathic, sensitive friend, a gifted artist, taught me about energetic boundaries. I still carry
two of her lessons with me: "your luminous body (the energetic layers we each have, extending beyond the border of our
skin) is yours, and just like your physical body, it should be
protected," and "your sensitivity is also a gift. Do not shut the
world out. Find a harmonious state you can walk life with." I
took her words in. I could not bear feeling the intense emotions of everything around me.

Finding a harmonious state took time. It was easier to turn off
my sensors than find a balance. But then, turning off my sen-

sors was the opposite of what I wanted to do. It meant turning off me. I had done that for too many years. So I explored ways to balance. Sometimes more successfully, sometimes less. I found that nature was the best source for the harmony I looked for. The trees, the bushes, the grass, and flowers. The rocks, the sand, the sea. The Earth. They absorbed all the energetic noise around them, such as other people's emotions. Creating a container to breathe in. Be. Connect. Focus on my wholeness. And for others to focus on theirs. Often, I was not even really outside. I was just looking out the window at the beautiful view of the fields.

I felt whole when I met kind people. Warm-hearted and open. Pure people, to whom I will forever be grateful, people who, from their eyes to mine, from their hearts to mine, were so pure they could see my essence and reflect it back to me. Helping me get a glimpse of it myself.

After the door to the academic world and teaching closed, and with the notion that one "must" do something, for some time I contemplated becoming a death midwife. One who compassionately walks with those about to cross over and complete their life cycle. Following my personal adventure of almost dying, I knew death personally. We became friends. I no longer feared it. The surrounding light one goes to when moving on is so magnificent, I was ready to die daily, as long as I could still return. I saw how my story positively affected those crossing over and their family members. Then, my grandma reached the end of her life, and I received the gift of being by her side in those precious and sacred last moments.

However, undergoing death midwife training frightened me. It was intensive and was to take place in hospitals. And I was still wounded myself. So as a way of exploring this path, I started volunteering in a young adult department in an assistant living facility. I went there once a week, sometimes every other week, for only an hour or two. I guess a mirror is something we constantly need in life, as those living there reflected what could have been. What could have been if the doctors had not managed to do such a great job in the emergency operations. What could have been if I had had a severe brain injury. What could have been if I did not have a loving family who was able to care for me while I was recovering. Those beautiful, pure souls living there saw me as just me. They were thrilled with my mere presence. The definitions I used to carry had no meaning for them. My slow walk was like theirs. We would look into each other's eyes and smile from our hearts. I came for them, and in turn, they healed me, filling me with soul gratitude.

I felt whole when I accepted what I knew for a specific moment and followed it, even in the tiny moments of life. It was making the right choices regarding what I ate, listening to what I knew about my ability to digest. It was listening to my need for rest. It was taking a clear look at the amount of energy I woke up with in the morning compared to what I had or wished to do and acting accordingly. Sometimes, it was also about allowing myself to speak out, even if I was not the one doing anything in our house or caring for my daughters. When I followed my inner feeling, gut feeling, intuition – we call it by many names – and acted and responded to life in ways that were congruent with it, my heart expanded, my whole body expanded, I got closer to the feeling l carried from my visit to the dimension of LOVE. I felt pure joy, I felt physically better, and I was able to be with and around my daughters calmly. To be present. When I let the noise of the world – or, even more, my frustrations – take over, my heart shrank, my body contracted, and I did not feel well physically, resulting in my trying to hide, distancing myself from any connection. It was so systematic and consistent that I could not ignore it, and neither could my family or close friends. I learned to listen to what I knew and to watch for my guiding signs. And the more I did, the more I opened, the more moments of divine LOVE I had here on Earth.

When I recovered and searched for my answers to motherhood, I was not aware of it all happening. I am much smarter with the power of hindsight. While finding my way, I was also frequently focused on being absent, my disabilities, my dependency on others, and my very ambivalent and inconsistent relationship with my daughters. One day I was next to them, the next I was again in the hospital for another operation. In the morning, touching me gently was fine, but as the day progressed, I would jump at their touch, making them very confused. At times, distancing myself was an attempt to respect their rhythm, respect the amount of connection they asked for. Reflecting, I sometimes wonder which part of it was right, and which was another excuse. I was not aware of the shedding, nor that the light was pushing the dust off of me. That things were evolving, and my relationship with my daughters was shifting. I often felt stuck. This process, of revealing deep parts within, of emerging out of the cocoon I was unaware I had created, was a prolonged process of accumulating many moments of wholeness. A process of trial and error. Lots of errors. Of searching for my way within my physical limitations. Within my inability to fully participate in taking care of my daughters' needs.

Despite my many physical limitations, my lack of guiding self-definitions, my dietary constraints, and my search for my way to becoming my daughters' mother, I felt better with myself than I had felt in years. It was my soul that felt good. It was my being. I was walking towards who I am, who I came here to Earth to be. Not that I had any idea at that stage what it meant, what I came to learn, or what service I am to offer. It was the inner feeling. It was the mere motion. Even if it was still only at the peeling stage. I felt the expansion, the tranquility, the light within me, the unconditional love, the lack of judgment, in the here and now of my every day.

Like a flower growing and developing, then suddenly blooming without notice as a moment joined a moment, and moments of wholeness started to accumulate, the answer to my wish of sharing the LOVE I experienced with my daughters bloomed. I was given the answer to how to share this LOVE with my loved ones here on Earth. To the way of guiding my daughters to feel this way in their lives. To my role in their lives, the one I can provide, even when not participating in the caretaking. The way to share the profound experience I had in my NDE. The way to have my daughters know that pure LOVE does exist, and that they are made of pure LOVE. Accepted. Beautiful, just as they are. It is not by sharing with them mom's story or telling them how beautiful they are and how much they are loved every night. Not that these things are not important. They are. Very much. It is by having my daughters live their light. There is only one way for each of us to live it on Earth, and that one way is to be us. Purely us. Not us as our culture, society, and family teach us. Us as in our essence. Us as in our deep inner knowing. Our soul's knowing.

That knowing that allows us to walk the path we wished for before becoming.

Guidance to a Basic Shamanic Journey

Shamanic journeying enables an intentional reach for information, knowledge, perspective, and guidance. While journeying is traditionally accompanied by drumming or rattling to facilitate the change of brain waves, journeying can also easily be done sitting quietly, when resting in bed or with open eyes.

There are numerous books on shamanic journeying; the guidance offered here is intentionally simplified.

Preparations: Find a quiet space to sit or lie comfortably. You can light a candle (you don't have to) or prepare crystals or anything in your surroundings to create a sense of ceremony.

Prepare a clock that you can set for ten minutes.

Relax: Focus on your breathing. Gradually slow your inhale and exhale. There are no rules on whether you should breathe in or out from your nose or mouth, nor on the pace of your breath. The pace should fit your abilities and who you are. Breathe comfortably, gradually slowing down and sensing you are relaxing.

The Journey Steps:
Set your clock to let you know ten minutes have passed. When you become experienced, you can journey for longer.

Close your eyes and:

1. Imagine standing in a place in nature that brings a sense of safety and relaxation. Preferably a place you know from this lifetime.

2. Explore this space. Smell, touch, look around, listen, and sense.

3. See yourself sitting down on the earth and closing your eyes.

4. Notice what you see or hear, what images emerge, and how they evolve. Trust.

5. View what comes up for you until the story unfolding comes to an end.

6. When your ten-minute alarm goes off, see your story come to an ending. Most likely, that will happen even earlier. If you went somewhere other than the safe and relaxed place in nature where you started, imagine yourself returning to it.

7. Express your gratitude for whatever came.

8. Take a deep breath and open your eyes.

9. Make sure you are fully grounded back in your physical reality. If you are unsure, you can move your body and name (out loud) several objects around you, identify smells and feelings, or see yourself sending roots deep into the ground.

You can write down what you see or hear; this could be as simple as sensing the soft breath of the wind, the warmth of the fire, the enveloping of the earth, or the healing sound of water. It may be realistic, or symbolic. You may meet your higher guidance or travel to other dimensions. Most importantly, don't expect, and allow yourself to just experience.

It is fine to fall asleep on your first try, not experience anything, or sense your body relaxing. Journeying serves each of us differently, and if this tool is indeed for you, you will develop your abilities with time. Many intuitives journey without knowing this is what they are doing.

Download a guided audio version of this journey at www.efratshokef.com

Sprouts of Love

ONCE UPON A TIME, *along the river of time stood a human. Was he a man? Was she a woman? The edges of her figure were somewhat blurry. She seemed much taller than average. He appeared almost transparent to the naïve eye, covered with soft, flowing, feathery "clothing."*

The human started to walk downstream. And the more she walked, the more she took form. For some time, he played, trying to have his hair short, trying to grow it long, shifting from one body structure to another, playing with the color of its skin. The more she walked forward, the finer were the details until a beautiful, dark woman emerged. Her hair falling down to her legs. Her green eyes sparkling. Her hands carrying light.

She thought it was her time to jump into the water that would carry her to her new life. But the river asked her to wait.

"There are some more details you need to decide on," the river told her with no words. "You cannot come in yet."

She sat and looked around, and there, on the other bank, were images of people walking. All kinds of families she could be born to. Single people, couples from both sexes or from one, so much variety and so many combinations. She was overwhelmed. The river raised its water and pointed to the far right.

"What do you think about those over there? Sitting together by the old tree?" It asked her.

She looked and felt her heart open. "Yes. Those," she replied.

"It is not going to be easy, you know," the river said, opening a screen-like surface before her eyes.

"You must look," it said.

The woman did not want to look. The pictures she saw were unpleasant. But she did, as she had to make the best choice possible. Then the river ran the images forward, and the woman could see how her life would evolve with that couple by the old tree as her parents.

"Yes," she said.

"Are you sure?" The river asked.

"I am," she replied and wanted to jump in.

"Not yet," said the river. "There is one more detail to go over before you flow into your new life." A book of shimmering light came down from above. "Nothing to do," said the river. "Just look for the last time, so that you remember what you asked for in this lifetime. So that you awaken your heart to the path you asked to walk."

The woman looked. Her eyes filling with tears of gratitude for the reminder. She had been so occupied with the creation of her temporary form, and her choice of Earthly parents, that she had almost forgotten. She gathered the words of light coming out of the book and brought them into her heart. Then she sat quietly.

And while she was sitting, her form became smaller and smaller, until she was no more than an egg, an ovum, immediately after it met its sperm inside of her human mother-to-be. Love started to sprout.

I started to remember all that I had forgotten. An inner knowing that I am more than my physical form. I was remembering who I am in my essence, and what I had asked to experience, learn, and do in this lifetime. Why motherhood was so important to me, both as part of my personal journey and the service I am to bring: sharing the learnings of my search for motherhood. The teaching of this extraordinary and unique kind of unconditional LOVE, and the journey parenting takes us on. I recollected the seeds planted within me for this journey. Remembering who I am. Remembering I was one with the mountains, my truth, and the truth hidden in each word. Remembering how it is to feel true joy and see beauty. Remembering how it is to be LOVE. How to love others. How to let others love me.

I was remembering me. Remembering the essence we all are – beyond our physical definition. Remembering all that I had entirely forgotten, for over three decades of my life, unaware I had forgotten anything. Living my life as if it was whole the way it was. Yet, often feeling those little hinting discomforts, indicating I was not precisely following my soul's path. Knowing something was not right. I had so deeply forgotten that I needed a huge fire, inviting a physical reorganization together with the doors that opened in my NDE, to clear my life, to enable the little spring of water that I am to start flowing. To remember.

I forgot that when I prepared for this life on Earth, I generated a blueprint of what I wished to experience and learn and the service I was to bring. I forgot that as part of this blueprint, as part of my sharing in the circle of soul-human-Earth life, I chose the parents I wished to be born to, which sperm and egg were to meet to create my vessel, my body. My mother and my father, who I felt would enhance all that which I wished to do here, during this journey on Earth. Souls I have a reciprocal relationship with, my presence enhancing their journey, just as theirs enhances mine. I forgot that in choosing parents before becoming, I inherently also agreed that at some point, I might also serve as a parent, a mother. Agreeing to this by the mere decision to come. I forgot that when a soul chooses its parents, the choice carries expectations for behaviors, experiences, events, and intimate and close relationships. Moreover, I forgot that when I chose my parents and carved out my expectations from them, I also agreed to those who might come to me one day, those who will choose me as their mother, to have such expectations from me too. I forgot.

My seeds, buried deep within me, forgotten from times past, needed an earthquake to awake. One that invited a new landscape to emerge, the reorganization of my body, together with a new perspective on life itself. For many, NDEs are an initiation. For me, it was an invitation. Unlike earlier invitations

I had felt, the NDE could not be ignored. I could not bury my head in the ground like an ostrich pretending nothing had happened. The seed within me awakened. Then, I needed to say multiple YES's to the inner call for my seed to grow. Sometimes resisting, slowly feeding it with the sacred moments of drifting to light, with intentional journeying back to the memories of the NDE to fully capture the experience and its teachings, and journaling – putting it in ink on the page as a witness. Until I could walk this truth that I am, share it with my family and friends, and share it with you here.

There are many reasons why I forgot. There are so many reasons why we all forget. Often, the mere forgetfulness is better for our journey on Earth, enhancing our experience here in all its facets. I, mostly, would rather not know of tomorrow's surprises. I try to focus on each specific day, often, just on one particular hour. The specific challenges a day brings, and if there are none, and it is quiet, I try to avoid thinking further and just relax. As parents, most days, focusing on the now is more than enough. Sometimes it works. Sometimes the "what if's" and the plans take over. Still, similarly to many of us in these transcending times, I did need to remember. I needed to remember that I was LOVE and so was everyone else. I needed to feel being LOVE in every one of my broken bones, in each of my torn muscles, all over my physical body, down to the depth of every cell, so that I would know to recognize it within my physical form.

I needed to remember the subtle essential essence of parent-child relationships. The subtle essence that would define me as my daughters' mother, even when not performing any expected "motherly" behavior. To remember the choices I had made and the expectations carried with them. I needed to awaken to the memory of choosing my parents and my agreement for souls to choose me as theirs. Then, within my desperate search for a small niche in which I could find my motherhood for my daughters, beyond the care they received from others, my heart slowly started to recall what these expectations held. To delve into their deeper meanings, into the spiritual depth of parent-child relationships. At this stage of my journey. It was yet to be about answers, as seems clear when I write to you now. I was also yet to understand that this quest I was on was not only for me to find my motherhood but also for me to write about these learnings and share them in additional forms. Initially, it was about the questions. And within the uncertainty and the search, I was starting to find a possible direction to fulfill those promises I realized I probably made to my daughters, even before my daughters chose me to be their mother.

Within the shattering in our lives, broken, wounded, confused, and not functioning, I wondered why my daughters chose me. Did they know before coming that there was the possibility of a car crash and the challenges it would bring to our family's life? To their upbringing? What were their expectations of me? Were these expectations spiritual? The understanding that there are spiritual aspects of parent-child relationships filled me with the hope that there is a reason for me to be in their lives, there is a reason for my return to my fractured body, a reason for me to heal, an answer to my prayer of being their mother. Once those understandings started to set in my heart, they first brought changes to the way I perceived my parents. If my daughters chose me, that means I, too, chose mine.

My parents were always loving. They were present. I could always depend on them and trust them. My family was home. It still is. I was privileged to always have a safe and nourishing place to come back to. They would always encourage me and support me in my choices. Together with that, as in any relationship, we also had our challenges. My parents are both the children of Holocaust survivors. My grandparents all had their epic stories of how they survived. One of my grandmothers shared her stories with the grandchildren when we were old enough. She managed to get her family to escape from Vienna,

Austria, with the help of her high school friends. Friends, I, too, had the honor to meet many years later when I accompanied my grandmother on a visit to Vienna. They all stayed in touch until they all slowly continued on. In that meeting in a cafe, there were over ten of them, chatting like they were still teenagers. My other grandmother never spoke of it. Her memories were horror stories and too painful. She would focus on the little happy things – like us, her grandchildren.

Spoken or not, our parents' trauma affects how we are raised. It existed within my family and in the social-cultural narrative of Israel, where I grew up. Both silently affected how my parents grew up and how they raised my two brothers and me. My home was a secular Jewish home. Traditions were valued. But in my family, the presence of a God, or any other greater existence, was dismissed – as Holocaust survivors and second-generation survivors focused on rebuilding their families, there were no conversations about the existence of God, Spirit, or other life mysteries. If there was any inner talk or conversation among the adults on these topics, we children never heard of it. It's not like that in all families. Each family has its unique dynamics. This was mine. So while my parents were my trusted source for nearly everything, they were not so for anything related to the energetic and spiritual aspects of our world. Guidance I desperately needed as a child and as a teen.

The recollection that I chose my parents, just as my daughters chose me, was striking. Moreover, that meant that they, too, are made of LOVE, inhabiting a human body. They, too, like everyone, are much more than what is seen or experienced in our physical, literal form of being. It was an understanding that took me time to digest, especially as so many of us, and so many from the generations of our parents and grandparents, live with so many wounds. Wounds from their childhood or Earthly experiences in this lifetime. Wounds carried down for generations, cultural constraints, and limiting beliefs from their families and past social and cultural traumas and conventions.

We are all made out of LOVE. This is a knowing I walk with since my NDE. A clear knowing. Unquestionable. Each and every one of us. We all also have the opportunity to stay as we know ourselves here or choose to walk the LOVE that we are, which means healing whatever stands in our way and releasing the binding constraints we carry. This is possibly one of the hardest choices for us to make, and it is a challenging journey to set out on. Walking as healthy as we can, in all facets of our being, is a choice. We can choose to heal ourselves and the wounds we walk with, even if the source is our parents. We can heal our ancestral lines and the traumas carried in our families and cultures, even if only to free ourselves and our children from the memories and energetic inheritance no longer serving us. This is partially why I perceive my NDE as an invitation rather than an initiation. For me to accept this invitation fully, and walk the wholeness, beauty, and acceptance of LOVE that I experienced in my NDE here on Earth, I too needed first to choose to heal deep wounds. Many I had no awareness I was carrying. Wounds that limited my perception of others. Wounds that derailed me from my ability to create. Limiting cultural beliefs of what is accepted and how a woman behaves, including many bounded perceptions of what makes a mother. Deep and true healing is an ongoing journey. I think I am done, and a few weeks later, I become aware of another element binding me and asking me to heal it. I work hard to heal what comes to my awareness. Any wound I manage to heal helps me walk closer to my true essence. Some of the wounds I heal may also relate to my daughters, freeing them from the task of healing that wound themselves.

Realizing I chose my parents, I suddenly had a new lens to understand my childhood challenges and the lack of guidance I felt for anything beyond what can be sensed with our five physical senses. A lack that now drives me to provide this guidance to other young humans. A lack I would not fully understand if I had not experienced it myself. Walking a spiritual path and agreeing to see beyond what I can see with my physical eyes were also abilities I needed to choose. If I had grown up in a family that practices these, it would have been easier to embrace such skills. In my personal path within this lifetime, I needed to choose, so apparently, I asked to come to an academic family and environment, allowing me this option of choosing.

Seeing it all as my choice and as a mutual, reciprocal journey between my parents and me seemingly erased all the colors on the page and refilled the same pattern of my childhood with entirely different colors. Colors of gratitude. Colors of much greater love. I had good colors in my initial drawing. And still, they all transformed, becoming so bright. So whole, multidimensional, and deep. My love for my parents took on a whole different shape of acceptance, honor, and respect for their individual journeys, life choices, and the mutual journey we are on. Realizing that they, too, are on a journey, making choices, and growing. These understandings, stemming from my heart, implanted new roots, growing new stems and branches, lightening our relationship, while allowing it to transform and continuously grow.

This process of remembrance was a delicate dance of observing, journeying, and awareness. And from this dance, in a light, subtle motion, the memory of our soul expectations – the most fundamental agreements between parents and the souls coming as their children – gradually became apparent. I would find myself writing about them in my journal. Words and explanations would just appear on the page. Wisdom about our reciprocal soul expectations with our children – a shared promise of LOVE. An answer to a question I was unaware I had asked when I invited all the mothers in the circle, four days before the car crash, to share what motherhood means to each of us.

We all made this promise of LOVE. I did. I promised that I, as one of my daughters' parents, whom they had chosen to guide them on Earth, would do everything in my power to allow them to be the beautiful LOVE that they are. I promised them I would keep the delicate golden thread of LOVE that defines us strong and connected. I promised to guide them on how to dance this delicate dance of human life. The one that will allow them to live a full life on Earth within their dense bodies, while not losing the sense of who they truly are, their essence, and the journey they came here for, like I did.

Our parents, Earthly ones, made this promise to us. We made this promise to our future children long before we were ready to have them. They made it to their future children too. Loving our children, and being the parents they all need us to be, is about this guidance in the dance of life. A dance of motion, ripples, in all stages of their development. A dance that will allow them to consistently know who they are and live in their essence.

This was the answer to my quest. To a way of sharing my experience of divine LOVE, unconditional, pure, and embracing, with my daughters. An answer to what motherhood means for me. As I learned in my healing journey, when I am aligned with my soul's knowing, even in life's very little moments, such as what I eat, who I meet, what I do, how I allocate my energy, or even what words I use, my inner feeling transcends to that feeling of divinity I felt in my NDE. I live heaven on Earth. In this sense, wishing to share my experience with my daughters is about guiding them to stay true to their paths and to who they are. My role in their lives, far beyond physical care, is to be their guide, the weaver of golden threads and Earthly ones, reaching a gentle hand to each of them. Each with the pattern she needs – its colors, directions, and composition – to stay the light she is, have her flame continuously burn, and walk the path she came to Earth to walk.

I think about my childhood, a good childhood, in a loving and nourishing environment, and I wonder. I look around at families I know. I look into our family and our home. So many of my daily routines as a child, so many daily routines in children's lives today, are about adjusting to social and cultural norms. Often, these social and cultural norms are simply what someone found effective in the past. Effective for survival. For order. A traditional part of the ceremony. It can be religion. It can be what is healthy to eat, or what one is accustomed to eating, because this was the type of food available in a different country and environment long ago. It can be about defining success and constantly preparing for it, forgetting to allow our children to be children. It can be about having to go to school, formal education being the only door to happiness. Or about not allowing our children to jump on the sofa, run around the house, express excitement or pain, or get dirty outdoors. These limitations are endless. We all grow up with such norms guiding our lives, and when we become parents, we often forget to ask whether they are still relevant. Are they our best practice of behavior, of reacting and feeling? Are they right for us? For our children?

Almost every day, I notice myself saying something, reacting to something, in a way that sparks these questions. I ask myself if I just played out a cultural norm. Then I ask myself if I agree with what I just performed. Yes, I want my daughters to be polite and respectful. No, they do not have to talk to or answer a question someone asked them if they do not wish to, even if it is an elder. Must they say a polite "thank you" when receiving a gift? Or is an authentic smile and excitement enough? Does everyone have to have an academic degree? Or should one follow their heart, providing for their families from an occupation that makes them happy?

I hope my daughters will always be discerning, using their judgment and intuition about what is right for them in each situation. If I wish my daughters to be who they are, to walk in beauty, to dance the flowing dance of each and every moment of their lives, then every little element of life should be disassembled, examined, quieting the noise in each convention, each common way of doing things, leaving only what she needs. Delicately blowing accumulated dust off. This is not to say that social and cultural orders are not important. Nor that children should not be disciplined. Social order, as well as order and boundaries within our homes, are important to the extent that they serve the family or the community. I would personally much prefer that social rules were all flexible, like the oral traditions of indigenous cultures. Like the stories told from generation to generation, omitting details that do not fit the now, adding ones that do. Learning from its essence, discharging it from any energetic heritage it carries. Remembering only what needs to be remembered, releasing what does not serve any longer.

As a parent, I feel that when I focus only on the adjustment of my daughters to the social or cultural norms around us, often not even aware I am playing out something inherited from the past that maybe we should question, I deprive them of their true journey. It is like placing giant rocks exactly in their path. These rocks accumulate. If, as parents, we do not do too much damage, our children might find their way around these rocks at some point in their adult lives. Just like we, the generations of their parents, have been doing in our personal and spiritual seeking. Trying to find our ways around our rocks. Like some of us, if our children are very persistent, they might manage to move the rocks and clear their way.

My journey taught me that my role as my daughters' mother is to guide them to stay true to who they are. I share this role with my husband as their father, and both parents each have one hundred percent responsibility, regardless of whether the other parent is fulfilling their promise or not (which they might be, even if it does not seem like it). We must provide the guidance they need to live here on Earth, in a society, and in a specific region or culture, with a very alert, aware, and flexible mind. With thought. With an open heart. Our role is not to be the hindering force. It is to be the facilitating one. And when we facilitate their development to their true nature and their authentic journey, they will shine. They will be aligned in their everyday moments, attentive to themselves. They will walk softly, adhering to their essence. They will have the opportunity to be living heaven here on Earth.

This promised, expected, hoped for guidance in the dance of the soul life here on Earth includes both universal and specific aspects. The universal aspects are the expectation of every soul, regardless of her soul's plan and choice of parents, embedded in the mere choice to come. Just as we expect these expectations to be fulfilled when we come to Earth, our children, when choosing to come to us, expect the same. And the same will be expected of them once they become parents themselves. These are contracts of LOVE we all commit to, and we all expect them to be fulfilled. We all share this contract, regardless of the country, location, or cultural environment we will be born to. They apply to every soul, every parent-child relationship. Every soul coming to Earth expects this part of the contract to be entirely handed to her.

The specific aspects are the particular expectations of a soul for the parents it has chosen and the journey she wishes to have on Earth. It may refer to the parents' personality, character, place of living, and living conditions. It may refer to other souls already in their family apart from the parents, such as brothers and sisters and immediate close family. It may refer to the creation of events that will facilitate what she wants to achieve throughout her life. These agreements outline the conditions and challenges that the soul wishes to face along her journey so she can have the learning opportunities she specifically needs for her development and the conditions that will allow her to be of service.

These expectations invite each parent to be attentive from their hearts to their unique relationship with each child. To what their child asks of them. To their desire to live their essence. Observing both the child's needs and the teachings they bring to their parents. It is always mutual. These expectations differ from family to family, and between children within the same family, as the same family can often serve different needs and souls' wishes at the same time, making generalization impossible. As far as the specific aspects go, there are no two souls that need the same reaction, challenge, or conditions for similar learnings or service. In my family, this means that each of my daughters, even my identical twins, has different needs in order for her to be herself and walk her journey.

And in a reciprocal relation, each one of my daughters brings different teachings to us, her parents.

The universal part of the contract is shared and is similar for all three of my daughters, and as I understand it, for all the children of our world. Hence, it is the focus of the following chapters, as this is what I have learned from my journey to find the depths of being a mother to my daughters and my wish to share with them the LOVE I felt in my NDE. It is what I learned to be the preliminary aspects of what our children need from us for them to stay aligned with their essence. It is the response to the most basic need in our journey here, and I feel it is applicable and relevant to every parent-child dyad.

This agreement structure has always existed, but it was often neglected because the basic needs of survival came first, as is unfortunately still the case for many, many children around the globe. In these transformative times we live in, we are asked to remember who we are and what we promised. To guide our children in the subtle, delicate dance of their lives. Giving them the guidance they need to be the LOVE that they are so they can bring their enormous gifts to this hurting Earthly world.

Loving our children. Truly loving our children means creating conditions that will allow them to be who they are. It is, in parallel, about loving ourselves. Creating for ourselves the conditions to be who we are. If we are not true to our essence, it will be difficult for us to guide the ones we love most to be themselves. Most of us do not need to go through a major life crisis, such as a car crash, a loss, or a terminal or chronic disease, for that awakening or to set out on a journey to heal whatever binds us. We merely need to be attentive to our inner knowing and intuition, trust ourselves, attend to the small discomforts inviting us to look in, and bravely show up to the invitations the universe sends us.

There are many elements to the universal promise of LOVE. There are many elements needed so that we can guide our children in the dance of life, allowing them to fully participate in the physical life on Earth, while continually adhering to who they are in their deepest essence. Staying true to the LOVE that they are. In the next chapters, following a chapter focusing on the concept of spiritually aware (beyond religion) parenting and the invitations brought by the journey of parenting, I focus on three basic elements. Truth: what does it mean to be walking truth, and why is it a crucial factor for each of us, both children and parents, as we stay loyal to our journey and our essence? Attentiveness: what is attentiveness, and why must we create conditions that will allow our children and ourselves to be attentive to our inner truth? And finally, the element of Motion: what is motion, and how do even tiny steps we take towards ourselves play out in our hidden communication with our children when walking back to our essence, to being LOVE, to serving in the world?

Absent-present, present-absent. The beauty of these universal elements of the promise of LOVE is that I could apply them, and live them, even when I was more absent than present in my daughters' lives. That is because we all have both physical hands and the reaching hands of our hearts. A while before the car crash, the five of us went to a monkey-rescue park, not far from our house. While we were walking in human cages, with the monkeys able to "freely" jump around us, another family walked before us. The father and another child further ahead. The mother and the daughter, about seven or eight years old, walked closer to us. The two of them were not jumping with joy or having a great time like most people around. It seemed like a dark cloud was drifting above the mother. As children do, the little girl forgot in some moments, running to see the monkeys, and in others, she tried to reach out to her mother. At some point, the little girl got closer to her mother and reached out her little hand. To walk together. The mother pulled her hand away. The little girl seemingly choked for a short second and then walked back to the friendly monkeys.

This picture stayed alive in my mind for a long time. Although it was none of my business, that pull of the mother's hand from her daughter's hurt me, too. I wondered what happened and hoped it was resolved happily, their relationship warm, loving, and accepting. Then, I experienced what it means to be absent. How you can be so deep in your physical pain, the pain of the heart, a worry, or merely being tired, that you cannot notice that little hand reaching out to you. And the more lost you are from yourself, with the things that pull you down, the harder it is to keep your heart open to the ones you love most, your own children.

I wish I had known about the reaching hand of the heart when I was in the hospital and in those many challenging months recovering at home. Very partially present, mostly distancing myself and absent. For a large portion of that time, I was physically unable to reach out, sometimes not even to myself. The beauty is that even when physically unable, we can open our hearts and reach out our hands through imagination. We can imagine holding our little one's hand, sweet and soft. We can imagine dancing together and having a blast in a field of flowers. We can imagine sitting together and reading a book. We can be laying in a hospital bed and imagine baking together, playing a game they love. We can imagine how our child is climbing a tree or a large rock and have them see us look at them, saying, "You can do it!" Or we imagine being together with someone else, tucking our child in to sleep, singing them their favorite lullaby. Doing it at the usual time or even at a different time of day when we feel a little better, transcending time and space with our imagination. Every morning, even if we are at the hospital, or already at work, we can imagine that big morning hug, the cuddle, and the loving kiss. We can tell them, every day, how much we love them. Have a soul-to-soul talk, and have them share what happened today, the good, the challenges, what they learned, and maybe also their fears. Share what happened at home, share about their friends, their dreams, their passions. Of course, it is much preferable that this will all happen in real life. But sometimes it cannot because of real-life circumstances. Imagine with an open, loving heart, and it will all reach your children as if it is the reality. Meet them at their core need of knowing they are loved, cared for, safe, and worthy. That even if you are not by their side physically, their being will know you are by them – heart to heart.

Just as we can use our imagination to escape reality, just as we can use our imagination to be creative, write stories, and invent new products, it is also a tool for healing. It is more than imagination as defined by our modern perception. It transcends time and space. It is a tool for dreaming reality into being. And as parents, it's a tool to be used with love. To connect. To heal.

Opening to the Luminosity of Your Parents

When we embrace the luminosity of all beings around us, something within us shifts forever. This invitation may or may not allow you this experience; as with everything, it depends on where we are in our journey. It is essential to approach this exercise with a pure and open heart; otherwise, we will not allow ourselves to see the true luminosity of others.

Permission is required when looking at others. Would you like someone to look at your luminosity without your consent?

The following instruction invites you to observe the **luminosity of your parents** beyond their human form. The same instructions can be used to view anyone's luminosity – assuming that you have explicit permission from them.

We ask permission on two levels: first, ask the person explicitly, then, to make sure, ask at the soul-to-soul level. If your parents have passed on, you can ask only on the soul-to-soul level.

If your relationship with your parents is not a good one, or there is a language gap, and they will not understand what you are asking of them (for explicit permission, we need the other to clearly understand what we are asking them for), that means you do not have their permission!

In that case, I suggest you ask others, like your partner or friends, for permission. Seeing the luminosity of one, and another, and another, will help you accept your own luminosity, and that of your parents as well, even without directly observing them. See further instructions ahead.

Preparations: Assuming you received explicit permission, find a quiet space to sit or lie comfortably. You can light a candle if you choose, or prepare some crystals or anything in your surroundings to create a sense of ceremony (it helps, but again – you don't have to!).

Relax: Focus on your breathing. Gradually slow your inhale and exhale. There are no rules on whether you should breathe in or out from your nose or mouth, nor about the pace. The pace should fit who you are and your abilities. Breathe comfortably, gradually slowing down and sensing you are relaxing.

Steps:

1. Close your eyes and ask within your heart whether you can see the luminosity of your parents – the ones you chose to come to. If you are not sure you have permission to look at their luminosity (even if you received their explicit consent), you will hesitate. See this hesitation as a reflection that this might not be the best time to see your parents' luminosity. We always ask for permission, both explicitly and at the soul level. If we get it, we know. If we are not sure, we assume we don't have it.

2. If you got permission, within your inner vision, in your imagination, ask to see your parents' luminosity without their bodies, without all the external characteristics you know. Without the way they dress or used to dress, their favorite cup of coffee or tea, or their place by the table – just their essence. You might see them as a ball of light or a vague luminous being. Maybe an image of a flower, a river, or a mountain will come to you. Don't try to get more details. Stay with the first mythical image that comes to you and allow yourself to be surprised.

If you find this exercise challenging, maybe you don't have permission to look, and it is still significant that you tried. It takes time to recognize when we have permission and when we do not. Or maybe your relationship with your parents is heavily blurred by life experiences. Trust that you will be able to see their luminosity and your own at the right time, and know that, regardless of what you see in such an exercise, you, your parents, your partner, your children, and everyone else is made of pure LOVE.

Download a guided audio version of this journey at www.efratshokef.com

The Parenting Journey

MANY YEARS AGO, BY the river of time, hidden in the woods, there was a small house. The house had an entrance room, which was also the kitchen and the living room. In this room, there was one comfortable rocking chair. A dog sat by the fireplace. And in the rocking chair sat an elderly woman. She knits. She knits from wool. Wool that she sheared, cleaned, brushed, spun, and colored over many years. She knits in circles. Each round in a different color. Each round with its own distinctive pattern. She knits and knits until the rug becomes so weighty in her hands and legs that it is time to close it up. She then puts the finished round rug, folded on rustic wooden shelves, next to the entrance to her small house. She has made many rugs, and sometimes neighbors or others passing by purchase one. Her rugs are not simple. Those who see them, those who touch them, know so immediately. Love flows within each knot. Magic runs within each round. Each color holds a secret gift. Those who sit on her rugs are immediately flooded with the clarity of their being.

One day, after the woman finished a large round rug – full of different, vibrating, eternal tones of blue – and just before she sat down to start a new rug, she heard a knock on the door. "What perfect timing," the woman said to herself. At the doorway stood a younger woman with a basket in her hands, her face low and tired. The elderly woman invited her in, set a tea kettle on the fire, and gently asked, "How can I help you?"

The younger woman took out a small rug from her basket. The rug was faint in its colors and heavy to the hand. The younger woman looked at the elderly woman with a question in her eyes. They sat quietly.

"I did it all by myself. I sheared. I cleaned the wool. I brushed it. I spun the wool into thread. I colored it with natural colors from the Earth. I thanked the Earth. And still, this rug does not breathe. There is no motion in it. I cannot work it. How do you make your rugs? Where does their magic come from?" She stopped, choking on her breath, looking around the colorful, lively room.

The elderly woman sat quietly and looked deeply into the younger woman's heart. Then, she closed her eyes, placed her wrinkled hands on the younger woman's heart, and said, "You see, my child, in my heart, there is love. Your heart is full of sorrow, and the sorrow comes to your rugs." She paused and then asked, "What makes you happy?"

The younger woman did not know her answer.

"Leave everything here, and join me for a walk," said the elderly woman.

And so they did. They went into the woods, and on their way, the elderly woman picked some fresh fruit, and the younger woman took it with fear. And the elderly woman dipped her legs in the fresh stream's water and even splashed water around, and the younger woman self-consciously laughed a little. And they continued, and the elderly woman sat to rest under a tree and enjoy the magnificent views, and the younger woman sat by her side and started to breathe. And as soon as she started to breathe, she started to cry, and when she finished crying all that she had to cry for, her breath expanded, becoming wide and full. And once she was able to breathe, she understood.

Since that first meeting, the walk they took together, the crying, and the expansion of breath, the younger woman often visits the elderly one. They laugh together. They knit together. They weave light and love into their rugs.

Being a parent is one of the most beautiful elements living on Mother Earth provides us. It is a journey of connection and love like no other Earthly love. Is any parenting experience also a spiritual experience? Yes. I believe so. And it is also about the choices we make regarding how we wish to walk our parenting. Choice, awareness, and intention are the elements that transform our parenting into a journey of reciprocal growth and allow its spiritual essence to envelop us.

Although it did not feel like I was given any choice during my NDE when I had to leave the most magnificent space I have ever visited in this lifetime, looking back, I know it was also my choice. A choice embedded in the blueprint I wrote for myself for this lifetime, the learnings, teachings, and the life dance and growth I wished to experience. In retrospect, I understand that my grandfather's urgency during those moments of heavenly grace was about my body's ability to survive without me in it. Time in between dimensions flies differently, a few Earthly moments feeling like a few days. As soon as I received the message that I must return, I was already floating backward until I felt like I fell back into my body and its overwhelming physical pain. So unlike the beauty and serenity of a second before.

"Why did I return?" I asked myself repeatedly for many weeks, months, and years. I knew I had asked to be my daughters' mother, but I also knew there must be something else from early in my recovery. Some possibility was awaiting. Service to others. An embracing of ancient knowledge and my own soul's journey. Beyond time. Beyond space. Have I found that secret meaning? Even with the writing of this book, a task on the list of things I wish to do before I die again, I am not yet sure.

Parenting. My desperate search for what would make me my daughters' mother set me also on a profound journey to myself. Not only to the mutual dance with my daughters, my husband, and all of us as one family, but also into me, as an individual. From awareness of my needs, challenges, and behavioral patterns and perceptions no longer serving me to profound healing of patterns I walked with, past life wounds that affected my being in the here and now, and ancestral heritage that asked for resolution. One cannot walk their true path without those around them, at least partially, doing the same. My daughters' ability to grow into who they came here to be will be challenged if I don't do what I need to do. So I try.

Taking responsibility where I can. It is a continuous process, as we are constantly growing, changing, and meeting ourselves in new challenges. Our river – mine, my husband's, that of each of our daughters – bends and curves, needing to adjust to its now.

What defines us as parents? Mothers? Fathers? Significant adults? And what is it about this journey of parenting that is so significant? So meaningful that I could not let go of this role in my life? Was it only about my daughters? Was it possibly also about the chance to restart my life? Does being a parent serve me as much as it serves the ones I parent? While there is an embedded silent element of hierarchy within the concepts of parenting, mothering, and fathering, our spiritual relationship with our children is mutual and equal.

The dictionary definition of "parenting" is "the act of raising/rearing/bringing up a child." "Spiritual" is defined as "relating to deep feelings and beliefs" and "of, relating to, or consisting of spirit or soul, as distinguished from the physical nature." Following my parenting journey, and in light of all the questions shared in earlier chapters, I would like to suggest a new definition of parenting: *the nurturing, guidance, and care of souls arriving on Earth until they become independent, present, and able in their own physical bodies.* In accordance, defining spirituality as *the manifestation of one's soul's journey in their life here on Earth, in form, in a physical body.* These definitions incorporate our relationship to our soul, our spirit, and our higher guidance, together with our Mother Earth holding and nourishing us. Thus, it focuses on our manifestation within our body, within our physical reality, not by leaving or quieting it down through meditations, journeying, and the like. Hence, spiritually aware parenting is the *act of guidance and care for souls arriving on Mother Earth, creating the conditions for each soul to grow its physical vessel and spiritual conduit so that it can walk the path it asked for, manifesting its soul's journey.*

These words were precisely carved, like the wondrous beauty of a flower. All elements, from its roots to its leaves, petals, and stamens are significant and crucial for its structure and beauty. "Souls arriving on Earth." These words capture the acceptance that we are more than our human form. To some extent, I always knew that and walked with this understanding all my life. With that, I do not recall myself thinking about it or exploring this notion deeply, as many people I know have. Sometimes, when someone close passed on, I would find myself comforting the grieving with an unforeseen knowing that their loved one is close by, existing in a different unseen form.

Then, following my NDE, I returned with no questions: we are beyond our physical bodies, which are temporary vehicles. And more, our cells are made of pure LOVE.

We "arrive." We are not sent. There is a choice embedded in each soul's journey to Earth. We may have had our questions before coming. We might have been encouraged to come at this specific time. Maybe past experiences frightened us a little. Possibly, some of us regretted our choice at the last minute or when we met the circumstances we chose to come to. Yet. We all chose. This also means we each have a reason for being here. And there is deep, profound meaning to the journey of each and every individual.

"On Earth." Earth, in this sense, is much more than a place, existing among other planets and dimensions of reality. Earth is our source of nourishment and safety. And if we let it, a sense of never being alone envelops us with its LOVE. Sadly, many of us forget that early in our lives. Most of us strongly feel a deep connection with the Earth as soon as we are out in nature. Many often feel this just by connecting with their house plants. As humans, we need this connection to thrive, to remember who we are. It cleans so much of the noise of our modern world. It is not by mistake that we learn from indigenous cultures that the Earth is our mother. What do mothers do? What is their role in our lives? Nurturing, feeding, care? More?

Just as human parents and children dance a reciprocal, mutual, and shared dance, we have an invitation to dance with Mother Earth, holding us while we are here, momentarily living on its surface.

Hereafter, the guidance and care we parents are invited to provide those souls who choose us as their parents is also about the dance with Mother Earth. It is not just about education, networking, making a good living, living comfortably, or even values. It is about connecting and listening, learning how not to exploit the Earth but to respect and honor it, and most importantly, about knowing gratitude.

Returning to the second part of the above definition of spiritually aware parenting: *"Creating the conditions for each soul to grow its physical vessel and spiritual conduit so that it can walk the path it asked for, manifesting its soul's journey."* We all wish to walk the journey we planned before arriving. These journeys are well crafted. Then we are born into our physical body and forget. We forget much more than what we crafted for ourselves. We forget that we are LOVE. My NDE and my ability to easily journey to these magnificent realms are continuous reminders I am extremely grateful for.

Our role as the human parents to these souls includes creating the conditions they need to fulfill their plan. Nevertheless, what are these conditions? I repeatedly tried to figure it out. I asked myself, "How can I know?" We don't always know. Or even more, our chances of knowing are seldom. But, occasionally, something might happen, and we can get a glimpse. Altogether, while this may seem like a dead-end road, if you have read this far, you already know what I learned and am finding extremely important to share here: **The way to walk the journey we wish for is by being very attentive to who we are, to listen to the truth bubbling within us, to what we know to be right for us and to continuously evolve**. When we are aligned with our truth, we walk with whole joy, gushing out of us, merely by walking the journey we wished to. That's remembering.

While we can all adhere to the universal expectations brought by our children, knowing what specific personal conditions our children expect is nearly impossible. My identical twins are an example. They are very much alike, but still each of them need and ask for entirely different interactions with us, their parents. Each crafts for herself the experiences she needs for her own growth. Together and apart. All while growing up with the same age-appropriate needs, in the same family, and thus the same conditions. Here is a simple example: They are both good at math. Yet, one enjoys it and can thus advance independently, preferably in a quiet room. Her sister, who is just as good at math, would rather do something else than sit and practice. Meaning that doing her math brings an invitation for patience and sitting together, mainly by the kitchen table, which is the center of our home. A completely different variation on the same theme. Different conditions are needed to accomplish the same assignment.

This understanding that I cannot know their deep soul expectations first left me a little helpless. Then, while growing as a parent and embracing who I am, the realizations shared in this book enabled the rooting of my being here: setting an example by embracing my own journey. By taking, with two grateful hands, any opportunity for healing or growth that my daughters and other circumstances offer. As the more I am who I came here to be, the greater the chances I will unknowingly create the personal conditions they wished for me to provide in their journey. And reciprocally, every element in their growth that is aligned with what they wished to experience during their journey here provides me with another opportunity to walk my path as I wished to.

Before deepening our perceptive on the three universal elements of LOVE – Truth, Attentiveness, and Motion – in the three following chapters, let us explore and open our shared horizon a little further to the scope of our journey as parents and its elements.

Caretaking: Caretaking was, is, and always will be of crucial importance. Whereas in my months of recovering, I was unable to provide any caretaking, and was confused and frustrated from seeing others do what I was meant to be doing, we as a family were fortunate to have other significant adults, all their closest family, envelop our daughters with everything they needed: proper food, diapers, laundry (we used reusable diapers), and their daily bath. Playfulness in mud, trips to the playground, cuddling and hugs, building and crafts, and organizing a story, tea, or birthday party for all the stuffed dolls and animals. While I, their mother, for a long time was a baby myself, dependent on all of the above assistance.

Caretaking is not only about physical nutrition. It is also about the soul. Emotional and spiritual hugs, warmth, and safety are as essential and crucial as physical nutrition, warmth, and safety. We need both to develop into the humans we asked to be. Some layers of this expected care are universal. We all hope to be fed and given primary living conditions. In parallel, many elements of such care are not universal. They are very cultural, regional, or life-journey specific, such as a choice to be born to a family living in an area with fewer nutritional resources, adhering to the personal aspects of our agreement with those we chose as our parents in this lifetime.

Guidance: A second element of parenting is guiding our children on how to live here on Earth – leading our children through the manual of playing, reading, writing, learning, communicating, managing finances, and engaging with cultural traditions and nuance. All that we perceive as needed guidance for them to grow up and be independent adults. Many personal elements of our agreements with our parents are played out in this guidance. We aim to choose parents that will provide us with the learning opportunities we each look for. These learning opportunities often play through the personality and challenges of the parents we chose, the life circumstances we asked for, and the type of guidance we receive from our parents and others: significant adults, siblings, teachers, neighbors, or even the librarian.

The guidance on how to live here on Earth is also about caring for our physical body, our vessel. This includes what we eat, how to exercise, maintain hygiene, etc. While this may seem a universal and essential aspect to some of us, a quick fly above the numerous cultures of our world and the countless variations of families and personalities we can choose suggests that this may also be a largely personal element of our pre-coming agreements.

Lastly, the guidance of living on Earth is an echo of the invitation to a reciprocal relationship with Mother Earth herself. This consists of a profound invitation for our children to know gratitude, such as for the food Mother Earth provides. Not because a religious blessing is a convention but out of genuine appreciation for Mother Earth's fruits. It further includes allowing our children to cultivate their reciprocal relationships with the Earth, connecting to nature, the soil, and plants, and the health benefits its hug gives us humans.

Is there any difference between parenting and spiritually aware parenting when it comes to providing our children with care or guidance? The difference lies only in the awareness we walk our parenting with and the intention that guides our parenting actions. We can be guided by our convenience or by our awareness of our child's needs. Our limitations can drive us. So can our busy life, or what we perceive as our journey. Alternatively, we can allow a broader perspective of the shared journey that we walk together to take the lead.

Intention is an extremely powerful source. There is a substantial energetic difference between a meal cooked to have something to eat and calm our children's hunger and a meal cooked with the same ingredients but with the intention to nurture our family's physical body while expressing gratitude. Our words, parental choices, and daily actions carry a different symbolism and effect when done with awareness, choice, and intent. It is often about being clear of the desired long-term results. Eating well in childhood not only prevents potential modern diseases and guides them on how to nurture their physical body. It also keeps open their channels to communication with oneness, Source, Spirit, and their guidance. Thus, they have a choice to be connected or not, rather than being unable to connect because of their physical body's state.

Providing and teaching our children life tools can also take the same two roads. It can be about them being independent so that we, their parents, won't have to be their drivers and have more time for our work or hobbies. On the other hand, using almost identical life tools to raise independent children can also be about empowering them. This subtle difference in intent creates an enormous difference in the message conveyed. It enlivens them with trust and the knowing that they are not walking this life alone.

Creating the conditions for each soul that comes to us (whether biologically, through adoption, fostering, marriage, or becoming a significant adult for a child) to flourish is based on intention. It is one of the elements that transform our parenting journey from just parenting to allowing the spiritual nature of parenting to guide us as well. It is not about withdrawing or subsiding those elements of physical caretaking and guidance about living on Earth. These are extremely important. It is about acting it all with deep intention. An intention to see, feel and know. An intention to accept and transform. An intention to respect the shared journey and, while walking it together with each of our children, to see the teachings they bring to us, as well as their needs and opportunities, thus creating the conditions that we all need to walk the journey we asked to. To learn and achieve what we came here to accomplish, for ourselves, others, our communities, and the Earth.

Looking back at my years of being a parent, nothing in life made me grow so much as the presence of my daughters within it. The absent times as well as the ones in which I am present. As parents, we each get a private teacher, or in my case, three amazing teachers. It is an ever-evolving journey. As children grow, they continuously present new challenges and opportunities for growth – both ours and theirs. Our reciprocal role is to say yes to the invitation and grow as well.

For me, loving my three teachers means that I try to listen with all the senses I have, five and beyond. Listen to what they need physically, emotionally, mentally, and spiritually. Listen to the direct and subtle guidance they provide. Every day, I try to accept their invitations for me to be my essence. To walk my path. They are always the greatest motivation to recover, heal, and become.

Since they were babies, my daughters expressed anxiety when too many people were around. One would express discomfort when held by others. Another started crying when it was noisy or crowded. The third would be drained after any activity with too many others. They all carry this gift of sensitivity still. Experiencing their request of us, their parents, was challenging at first. We could not go to many social or community events. We live in a very social-cultural environment. We were criticized for being overprotective when trying to listen to their request and learn what was right for each and all of us together. We learned we had to limit the length of time we were with others. And then the car crash came and invited me to learn to meet myself as well. Our daughters bring the gift of being attentive to themselves. And by their needs and gifts, they ask us, their parents, to walk inward as well. To make conscious choices about where we go, who we spend time with, and our tolerance of noise or loud music that others enjoy. Embracing this awareness was as much for them as it was for me. I, too, needed to learn to watch my boundaries.

Spiritually aware parenting is an amazing element of our journey here on Earth. It is the invitation to become who we are, in our essence, with all our beauty. To be the LOVE that we all are so that we can guide our children by personal example. In a way, it is also a new opportunity. We grow up. We were shaped by the many conditions of our upbringing, along with our social and cultural environments. Hopefully, some of what we asked for before coming worked out as we wished it would. Possibly, some did not. When our children are born into our family, from our wombs or our hearts, they offer a second chance. A new beginning. We see their innocence, their beauty, and their clarity, and we are reminded of who we are.

I hope that now it is clearer what spiritually aware parenting means to me: *The act of guidance and care for souls arriving on Earth, creating the conditions for each soul to grow its physical vessel and spiritual conduit so that it can walk the path it asked for, manifesting its soul's journey.*

The journey is about manifesting on Earth within and from our physical body. This perception applies to our reciprocal relationship manifesting both our shared and separate spiritual quests within our shared lives. When we act and parent based on awareness, intent, and choices rather than because others are doing such and such, or some expert decided this is the right way for all children, we allow our shared journey, mutual needs, and wishes for growth to evolve in our lives the way each of us wished they would. It is parenting consciously, walking present to the moment and the invitations it brings to us – parents, our children, or both.

For many of us parents, spirituality takes form as part of a separate part of our lives. We try to meditate or journal for a few moments when our children are at school. We may try to practice mindfulness to evolve our presence and become more patient. This is all important. However, returning to the proposed definition of spiritually aware parenting, these are only tools that will hopefully help us become more conscious of the path we wished to walk, of who we are in our essence.

Bringing awareness into our parenting is a constant wakeful choice. It is about looking around and seeing, feeling, and knowing that what our child needs at that moment is to go home and have some quiet time, even if we carry the perception that it is essential to know how to socialize. It is relentlessly asking, what is right now? For my child? For my children? For me? For all of us? By transforming the journey, we walk together into an aware journey instead of celebrating their 15th, 18th, or 25th birthdays feeling we missed some of the paths we wished to hike together.

Choosing to parent with awareness and intent, walking consciously, and turning parenting into a journey is what transforms parenting into a dancing quest. It is unlike any other journey life on Earth offers us. My daughters were and are my greatest motivation. It is easy to fall into the helplessness of daily intensity and let go of being aware. And that does often happen. But then, when it is also about them, I quickly rise. The realizations of my recovery, and the teachings of the NDE together with journeying, often push me to repeatedly leap so that I fulfill my promises to them. I walk with a deep appreciation for the gift they have brought to my healing journey. The profound understanding that the only way for me to have them share my experience of our energetic being, of being much more than their physical forms, of LOVE in its purest unearthly form here on Earth, is to create the conditions for them to flourish. For that to happen, I must walk the path they expected me to when they chose me as their mother. Reciprocal. Shared. Mutual. A dance of lights.

Intentional Parenting – A Journaling Exercise

Preparations: Take out a notebook or blank piece of paper and a pen or pencil. Approach this exercise when you have at least 15 minutes, as it usually takes us a few minutes to gather ourselves, center, and put daily concerns to the side.

If you would like, light a candle, or prepare other ceremonial elements around you.

Journal on these two guiding questions:

1. Create a list of activities, interactions, and reflections on your interactions with each of your children. It is important that you do so separately for each one. Then, ask yourself which items in your (hopefully) long list reflect intentional and aware parenting. This journaling exercise aims merely to take you a step forward into greater awareness of what motivates you in your parenting.

2. Choose one or two items from the list you crafted and journal, separately for each of your children, on the question: "What is my child asking of me in this behavior/interaction/activity?" Make sure you answer this question not only from your child's perspective – what is their need? – but also from your own. What growth could your child be offering you or inviting you to by behaving this way?

Truth

MANY YEARS AGO, FLOWING in the river of time, there was a barefoot child. On her face, a huge radiant, joyful smile. Her eyes shining with a glow that sparkled to the far distance. The child loved the soft touch of the green of her meadow when she lay on her back, gazing into the sky. Every morning she would drink the dewdrops from the grass, leaning against an ancient tree, standing tall in her vast meadow. The child and the tree humming together songs of love.

Innocent is the child, clear-hearted, and pure. She knows the now. Attentive to the details of her being. She speaks only truth, seeing pure beauty, goodness, and wisdom with her shining, luminous eyes. Dancing with the motions of her days.

One day, the child took an extended trip throughout her meadow, reaching its edge, seeing a different land ahead, until she reached places she had not walked through before. And while she was walking, the ground became scorched, rocky and dry, and fewer and fewer plants surrounded her.

Just before she was about to turn back, she heard the unexpected noise of banging stones. She looked to the distance, wondering about its source. It was then that she saw another child, appearing to be her age, sitting on a massive rock. The other child, with his head down towards the Earth, was distractedly trying to hit two stones together, one against the other in what sounded like a steady rhythm. His eyebrows were furrowed. Deep sorrow appeared within his eyes.

Our child wondered. Her heart was reaching out to that of the other. She walked closer and asked, "What happened to you? Are you okay? And what is this place?"

"Here?" Replied the other child, pointing to the many walking with their faces to the Earth around them, barely lifting his own. "Here is the place where the lost come to. Those injured in their heart." He moaned and whispered, "Those who have forgotten."

A few quiet moments passed by, and then the other child stopped hitting the stones he held and quietly asked, "And where did you come from? Has your heart been injured too?"

"No," our child said. "My land is very different." She hesitated for a moment, and then out of the depths of her heart, she said, "Come. I think you might like it better."

So they did. They walked together. They walked through the rocky and dry land. The sad child walking but not understanding his actions.

"Why am I following her?" he thought to himself. "This child's stories cannot be real."

But still, he walked, his heart pushing him forward, knowing that this strange child, with those shining, sparkling eyes, radiating to the distance, knew something. Remembered something he may have forgotten. Something deep within him started to tingle and awaken.

The green meadow started twinkling to them from a distance, and as they walked, they saw the flowers and the butterflies. They saw the dewdrops smiling at them. They saw the ancient tree, blissful that his friend had returned.

It called to her through the Earth, "Come, come."

As they reached the tree, the child with the sparkling eyes gave the tree a warm, loving hug. The other child thought of turning around. Then, she sat on the warm, nurturing Earth, sinking into its embrace. She invited her new friend to join her. The other child looked at her, full of doubt, but he hesitantly did, reaching his hands down to feel the grass. He was not so comfortable with the earthy, wet feeling. He then bent his knees and lay down on the Earth. On his back. It was all so different from what he knew before. He closed his eyes, dropping into the Earth. Weightlessness penetrated him, his breath became lighter, grace filled his heart, joy and happiness spread to all ends of his body, and he repeatedly mumbled: "How did I forget?" "How did I forget?"

Truth. The first of three shared universal promises we all made to our children. What is Truth and what is this Truth we forgot? Based on all that I have learned during my journey from the car crash to now, I know that all of us, when coming to Earth, know that we are LOVE and that we are made of light. The same is true for our children. When our children come to Earth, born out of our wombs, they too know. They do not remember, like us, their parents. They know. They know they are LOVE. Pure. Clear. Light. Weightless. They know who they are in their essence. They know the healing nature of the Earth and are not afraid to radiate their beauty. They are authentic, true to what they know and to how they perceive the world. That is the truth many of us forgot.

On a Saturday afternoon about two years after the car crash and the NDE, we visited close friends. We came in to find that almost everyone else had arrived. Kids were running all over the place, coming in and out of the huge garden, bumping into their parents sweaty and smiling, getting some water, drinking half of it, and disappearing somewhere on the other side of the host's garden. After an hour or so, another family arrived. They had recently had a baby. Their first. She was about four months old, held comfortably in her father's arms. Everyone's eyes were big, staring, admiring. Even most kids stopped running, standing near their parents, greeting their new friend with curious eyes. She hid in her dad's shoulder. Most of us slowly moved closer, tilting our bodies as if we so wanted to take her into our hands. As the afternoon wore on, she was not left alone for one minute. The kids held her tiny hands. The adults pet her softly, held her, and smelled her baby smell. That smell of a breastfed child that has eaten only clean foods in their short human lifetime. It was like that with my babies too. And twice as much with the twins. Identical and tiny. They used to constantly reach out their hands and somehow find each other. Deeply connected, as they still are these days, fascinating everyone around them.

Most people I know, adults and children alike, adore babies for their truth. We delight in their attunement to themselves.

Smiling at us for a moment, and in seconds, shifting their interest to something else, forgetting we exist. Joyfully taking one spoonful of mashed avocado and pushing away the next. Is it just entertaining? Amusing to us? Is their cuteness there just to appeal to and attract us to care for them? As part of our always reciprocal relationships, their truthfulness is also about us. Appealing to us because it turns "on" a forgotten button in our system. A button that, at some point in our life here on Earth, was switched to "off," and so many of us live entirely unaware of its existence. By their mere presence, with their softness, trust, and light, they draw delicate golden threads of remembrance into our hearts. As we too were once direct and honest. We, too, once knew truth, presence, and the connected nature of our being. We, too, once fluently spoke the language of truth. The truth of our hearts. Young children appeal to us not only because they are cute, and not only to encourage us to care for them, but also because they remind us of who we are, reflecting something we buried deep within ourselves. And by this reflection, this invitation to switch "on" our button, they magnetize us to their purity.

We all come from the unity of souls, and when reaching Earth, that unity, that oneness with all, comes with us. We are one with our mother. We are one with the family cat and with the family dog. We are one with the Earth, the plants, the rain, and the wind. We are one with the food and with our favorite soft teddy bear. We are both physically small, in a baby's body, entirely dependent on the physical care of our parents or others, and at the same time, we are equal contributors to the energetic vibrations around us. Wherever they are, children are present. They bend down to observe the digging ants, pulling us close, too, to be amused by their findings. On wet days, they jump into the rain puddles, and if not allowed, they concentrate on poking a stick into them, creating small ripples in the water. They touch the flowers and leaves and the trees we walk by. They are more than one with the ants, puddles, sticks, or ripples. They are the flowers and leaves. They are the trees. Until, because of Earthly, logical, important commitments, such as our wish to end a tiring day, to prepare a meal, or to deal with the laundry pile that is waiting, we hurry them up. By repeatedly hurrying them from their fascination, we unintentionally drop tiny, accumulating seeds of doubt, unseen to the eye, into their wholesome nutrition.

When we are born from our mother's womb, we know we are one with her, and we know truth. Within the truth of our hearts, there is no partial-truth, half-truth, white lies, or cutting corners. Knowing the local language when arriving in a new place is always beneficial. When our children arrive to us, it is more than wishing to come to a place that speaks a language they already know so that their adjustment can be more comfortable. Languages can be learned, and children are the first to see beyond languages and cultures and adjust to others and to new environments. Part of the silent promise we all make to our future children is to guide them in a way that would have them keep their essence's language – that of truth. The one they come with. The one defining them. If they are to be who they are, congruent to their essence and to the path they came to walk, they must be able to be themselves. We must be able to be ourselves. Being ourselves is not possible if we divert from the truth. Deep truth. The truth that can never become subjective. The truth communicated to us through our hearts. Not as outlined by facts, information from a "reliable" source, disinformation, or cultural and religious dos and don'ts. We must each be able to be authentic to who we are. Being ourselves is not possible if we go and replace the language of truth with another, as we adults often unintentionally teach them.

During my first few weeks at home, while spending hours on our purple couch or in bed, all of us adults tried to learn the new routine. Meanwhile, my daughters, although confused by my return and condition, seemingly accepted what was going on. They were in the now. Possibly led by their own inner knowing that it was all going to work out. But we, the adults, the so-called responsible ones, unintentionally imposed our concerns. My twins were just starting to walk. As part of their practice, they loved running in our small space. And if possible, then in circles, all three falling over one another, laughing from their hearts. I would get dizzy. They would fall on my legs too. Although it was a heartwarming and amusing scene to watch, I often felt it was better if I got out of the way, because when they would accidentally touch me, I would often jump because of the hypersensitivity in large parts of my left side, unable to control my reaction. Or, if I were less sensitive that day, and the touch was bearable, someone else in the house would jump for me with a loud "be careful!" So while they were in the now, we were communicating a lack of consistency. As part of my absenteeism, the easiest, but often heart-aching, solution was to stay away from those "running in circles" parties.

At that time in our family's journey, we were all carving our way through. Sometimes through fresh earth, easy to navigate. Often through unfamiliar territories of hard rock, moving through very small cracks. Sometimes, all of us were within the same stream, often splitting until our streams joined again. I was completely confused as to what was right. Navigating between what was before and an understanding that there are alternatives. Not yet grasping what exactly they are, nor finding words to express them. My heart, the new knowing I came back with, drumming within. Sometimes louder, sometimes other voices shushing it. Naturally, but with no awareness that this is what I was doing, I was communicating this confusion to my daughters. So were the other adults around. It was indirect and unintentional. We did not know what we know now. We all did our best. With that, the inconsistency was communicated. The confusion made its mark. Was I to be trusted? "She seems to love us and wish to get close, but then she jumps, and they tell us to be careful... and she is always in bed... and not with us." Were these their little thoughts? Are they my interpretation? So even after I was already better, less confused, clearer and more present as their mother in my new understandings, and starting to participate again in their care, trust had to be built. We all had to relearn how to follow our instincts, our truth. Let ourselves connect. Learn how to listen to the knowing of our hearts again. It often felt like I was adopting my own daughters. It took a long time until we all felt we were joining the same stream, calmly flowing on our way forward.

Within our lives in dense human bodies, we can identify "truth" in four different layers of perception. The first one is literal: that which is concrete, experienced by our physical senses. Everything is as it appears to be. I either walk with a walking stick or I don't, I have a cast on my arm or not, I leave the dining table soon after we all sat down or stay until everyone is finished. The layer of literal perception is the closest we can perceive "truth" as absolute and total. That is: one is either hungry or not. Either one is walking with a walking stick, or they do not.

However, there are many nuances even in humans' perception of the literal, and we often find ourselves experiencing these same concrete aspects slightly differently. Are two hours of resting during the day little rest? Or a lot of rest? Is reading together three books one after the other plenty, or not enough? Is my shirt plain blue, navy, indigo, or berry? Thus, even the literal can be experienced differently. With that, it is as close to concrete, "objective" reality as we might get.

Often a literal perception of an event or situation stays with us even after circumstances change. The concrete, literal elements become part of a memory. My daughters' literal description of me during my recovery, which focused on my cast, walking with a stick, and always staying at home and resting, continued as part of their description of me for some time, even when I was able to walk without a walking stick, hug them, and stay awake all day.

The following layer of perception is that of our thoughts as perceived in our minds and our emotions. Some would also distinguish between emotions and thoughts. I believe that in our shared understanding of truth, it is fine to relate to emotions and thoughts together. This layer is the "subjective" interpretation. What might be true for one may be perceived completely differently by another. While I was recovering, my family thought it would be really good for me to see friends and socialize. They perceived it as a healthy distraction, an encouragement to get back into life as we'd known it. I mostly felt that I'd rather not. Sometimes it was because I was uncomfortable being seen in my thin body and distorted figure. Other times it was because I was calculating my energy; changing from my home clothing into anything more took too much of it. I knew that a visit would take more of my energy than it would give me, and I had other priorities for using the little energy I did have, such as spending time with my husband or daughters. Sometimes it was because the visitors no longer aligned with the vibration I needed around me. Some would come back later, in a new version of our friendship, while others would continue on their own journey. The "reality" was the same on the surface – I barely left our house or saw others beyond my family – but my family's feelings about it and mine were different. Both their perception and mine were the "truth." Two somewhat different interpretations of the same situation. The example of what different psychologists and the stoma nurse recommended sharing with our daughters, described in Chapter 3, is also at this layer of perceiving "truth." Different minds see the same situation through different views.

Some shamanic traditions (see the wonderful book *The Four Insights*, by Alberto Villoldo, for more on these layers of perception), relate to two additional layers for perceiving our reality that are relevant to our understanding of truth: a layer of the soul's journey – the mythic – and the layer of the energetic. When we perceive from the layer of our soul's journey, we aim to look at the bigger picture. We interpret or understand an event by looking beyond the literal facts or the emotions and thoughts it evokes. My car crash was a literal car crash. Two cars, two women injured, a closed road, ambulances, and a helicopter. It sparked thoughts that ran from trying to understand what exactly had happened (who turned her car and in which direction, and how each car moved once we crashed) to thoughts of how to get well, how to choose the right medical interventions, and how to find my way back as a mother. It evoked all kinds of emotions within and around me: surprise, fear, sadness, pain, anger, confusion, but also amusement, calm, relief, forgiveness, surrender, and acceptance. All intertwined in the beautiful dance of life.

At the layer of my soul's journey, the car crash and the NDE invited me to reorganize my being at all layers of my existence. It invited me to experience LOVE. It taught me what LOVE is. Meaning was the truth wishing to be revealed. The car crash was an invitation to embark on a greater journey than the mere curing of my wounds. It invited deep healing. It was about grabbing my attention. It was about learning to hear, to sense, to feel, and to know *my* truth, my journey, and how I wish to walk it in this lifetime. This truth, my truth, is a very subjective, individual truth. In parallel, it is also our shared truth. When we each live by this deep knowing, by the embers of wisdom we all carry, our paths merge. They unite. When we unite, we reach the fourth layer of perception: that of being one.

This unity is pure energy, the essence of our being. It is what I experienced in my NDE. Oneness. Love. The one truth informing us all. That is the truth our children are born with. That is the truth they know before their upbringing in the literal, physical world, encompassed by many thoughts and emotions around them, push this profound truth somewhere deep inside them. This is the truth that we adults meet when we see babies – new arrivals to Earth. Their glow turns on those forgotten buttons within us. Fanning the embers left from our fire that stopped burning when we grew up, which are hidden deep within us. The embers of knowing our truth, sleeping within us, shining and glowing quietly within, are never fully extinguished. Always, always believing that their time to strongly burn and light our path can and will come.

Truth. The truth we all share. The truth of LOVE I encountered in my NDE is, for me, far beyond beliefs. There is a great deal of evidence today for various NDEs experienced by people of all ages, all ethnicities and races, from all around the world, practicing different religions, walking different life paths. These documented experiences have a lot in common. So much in common that it cannot be overlooked as coincidence or interpretation. These commonalities transcend literal interpretations, the dos and don'ts of religious, social, and cultural expectations. They transcend our thoughts, the interpretations of our mind, and our related emotions. They take us soaring. High into the possible. To the places where our seemingly different journeys, and our seemingly different truths, meet and converge into one truth. The truth of LOVE. The LOVE that we are. This is the deep notion of our children's language of being. The one guiding them upon their arrival.

As parents, these layers of truth challenge us. We are to guide our little ones to stay attuned to the knowing of their hearts.

To the connected nature of our source. To who they are in their essence. Then, in parallel, we are to guide them in living here on Earth. A very literal, physical, dense, and sadly often separated environment. Extremely different from the deep truth of oneness they bring with them. The natural, often, unintentional way to guide them is to help them forget, as I have forgotten. As most of the adults I know have throughout their lives. As, sadly, is still the guidance given to most children today. For me, that is opposite of all that I have learned. That is not LOVE. Accordingly, the questions stay open: How do we bring these different layers together? How do we both guide our children in their lives here, caring for them from the basic needs of their physical body to their emotional and mental needs, while also guiding them to stay true to their essence, to their hearts knowing, and their soul's path?

Allow me to try using a backward manner to show what can change in the parental guidance we provide. Starting from the opposite. There are so many examples in our lives in which we unintentionally bring our little ones to question the truth of their hearts. Examples that differ between families corresponding with their journey. It begins at a very early age. We offer our children various foods to taste. Some they like; others they don't. We can respect that. We can also insist we know better. We can communicate to them that they may be wrong about which foods make their tummy relaxed and full, making them feel good, and which foods do not make them feel good. They cry or try to communicate in some other way that they must have their diaper changed. That they are uncomfortable. We either listen or at least try to understand what it is that bothers them and act upon it, or we delay changing the diaper for whatever reason – because we want to save diapers for financial reasons, or because we have other things to do, such as answer a phone call or prepare the food they will want to eat immediately after being changed. Again communicating that we know better, weakening our child's knowing of themselves. Reducing their trust in their own truth of that specific moment. Moreover, it teaches the child that discomforts, in this case a physical one, are to be dismissed. When in fact they are a tool of communication with our soul.

We question our children's inner sense of truth in so many life moments. They do not feel well but do not have a high fever, and we have an important meeting that morning. We convince them that they can go to school instead of listening to what they are asking us for – to let their body rest, and possibly more, to realign, to connect, to be. We communicate to them that what they know for themselves – that they need to withdraw for a day from the busy world around them – is wrong. Something happens at work, or in our family, and we are sad. Our child, who recognizes only truth, grasping the energetic vibrations we come home with, comes to us and asks, "Why are you sad?" We tell them we are not sad, though we actually are. We excuse ourselves with reasons of their age, or that they do not need to know, it is not part of their world and so forth. But it is. Because we are their world. We could say, "Yes, I am a little sad today." We might share more and add, "I am sad because..." or say, "Yes, I am sad today, I am not even sure why." Friends want to come over, and we already have other plans. They hear us telling the friends that someone is sick instead of telling the truth that we have other plans.

We also confuse them with the meanings of important words. They receive a gift and must thank the giver. Is a smile enough? Is joyful immediate playing with that toy enough to show gratitude? Do we share with them our deep gratitude for abundance, for the people in our lives? Or do the words "thank you" remain empty, words to be said politely, unrelated to whether they are grateful or not? We ask them to apologize, often, when they do not yet mean it. With this, as with gratitude, we disconnect forgiveness from the true meaning it holds. The seeing of myself in another, of reducing our judgment, of acceptance, of unity.

The divergence from our deep truth penetrates every aspect of our lives. Maybe we trained ourselves this way to manage some crisis in the untruthful world we grew up in. Perhaps we were helpless as children, and the made-up stories we told ourselves helped us through it. We might have learned it from our parents, who were wounded and walked at a distance from their truth. Possibly we learned it as social convention, such as being politically correct and always being kind to everyone, making others happy. The thing is, no one is happy. Because deep down, at the layer of our souls, in our energetic fields, in our hearts, we all know how to distinguish between what is true and what is not. It is not necessarily a conscious realization but a mild, misunderstood discomfort. So in our minds, in our interpreting thoughts and emotions, if we are not communicating with our hearts, we might feel good. But within our hearts and souls, we always know. This is sadly the case for so many children and adults.

Crises, such as an illness within the family, the death of a loved one, divorce, or the loss of a job, are times of challenge. For many of us parents, if the situation permits and our children are not at the center of the crisis themselves, the automatic instinct is to "protect" them. We think we should not burden them with adult stuff or that they cannot understand, and it will frighten them. We sometimes lay it on their ability to perceive time. Most often, it is us who are not managing to deal with what is happening on a physical, emotional, or energetic layer and are thus unable to communicate it well to our children. So we either say nothing or we stick to dry facts, which are never a full, deep truth. We try to explain it to them partially, making up all kinds of stories, asking those around us who know not to talk about it around them. Sometimes not realizing that our child's friends hear about it from other adults talking.

When something is going on, our children know. If they are a little older, then they have already heard about things that happened in other families. Most of them have friends in class who live in two houses, and they have read stories or seen movies with orphan children as the main characters. In this way, way before they know in the literal, they know in their being. They know at the core of their energetic existence. They feel our vibrations. They know how we feel. They are one with us, and even if they cannot name it, they feel it. Hiding from them what is going on is saying everything is all right when it is not. That is not being honest. That is not walking truth. They know, always know, that something is going on. As they feel it energetically, they try to find explanations, making up creative stories going to the extreme, bringing disproportional fear into themselves and, at the same time, not having the adults, ideally their secret keepers, to work it out with. Moreover, the gap between what they know and what we communicate to them reduces their level of trust in us. When those tiny reductions in trust accumulate, they undermine children's validation of their truth, confusing them and distancing them from their inner knowing.

Being honest about a crisis, or about anything for that matter, is not about sharing all the details. It is about being honest that something is going on. Sharing details only at an age-appropriate level, and with personal adjustments that keep the specific child in mind. This could mean using a story that is aligned with the specific situation, keeping it honest and fitting to the truth. The wide truth of possibilities. No lies. No promises about matters out of our hands. No made-up explanations. It could be as simple as saying, "Yes, this is a very challenging time for us, and we are doing our best; there is nothing to share now, but if there will be, I will share it with you." Or "Mom has to go through some treatments in the coming weeks. We do not have all the information ourselves. It might take more time. We also wish we knew more." Or, "Yes, grandpa is not well, he is very sick, and it seems like his time to pass on is coming. I am sad. I will miss him." Often, the recognition that it is hard on us, too, that we are not ignoring their knowing, is enough to avoid the creative stories that can bring deep fears and confirm to them that what they know is truth. Sometimes being truthful is acknowledging that "I do not know," "I am not sure," or "Maybe

I got this wrong." Walking truth often starts with not trying to be anything we are not. Hence, not creating gaps between what our children know within and what we communicate to them at all layers of our being. Avoiding the accumulation of small dismissals.

Some children are more sensitive than others, usually born to at least one sensitive parent. Other children are either very persistent in their truth or are not naturally affected by every little divergence that we, their parents, make. The more sensitive our children are, the more they ask that we will be very attentive to their true needs, adherent to the truths they bring forth. For them, every divergence, every gap, is a shattering of their belief. A shattering of their inner knowing. Of their truth. Many such children are here on Earth, many more than most of us realize. Many of them, already close to their arrival, meet various life situations that dismissed their sensitive nature, questioned their knowing. Their truth. These situations taught them to hide their sensitive nature and dismiss what they know. Hiding it, ignoring it means they overlook a significant part of who they are. We, as parents, must learn to nourish the sensitive parts of our children, as we nourish their strengths, being aware of their delicate nature.

Many of these sensitive children have psychic abilities, such as an ability to see others' auras, an ability to communicate with their spiritual guidance, an ability to know what is about to happen, or deep wisdom, knowing the precise question to ask or the most accurate thing to say. We adults might not find this wisdom fitting to our expectations about what is appropriate for their age. When I was a teenager, there were a few months when I sensed when someone was about to die. It was frightening. I did all I could not to know. I felt very lonely just being who I am – a human with an ability to walk connected to the energetic field surrounding us. It made me close a door to myself, then need a car crash and an NDE that left me no choice but to walk through that same door. I often hear such stories from children and teens I now work with. It is their reality. And yet, they learn at a very early age that this part of their reality should not be shared, often not even with their parents. Not sharing often causes them to question these amazing, beautiful experiences they have, to question truth communicated to them through their heart and soul, and eventually to deny it, closing precious doors. Distancing them from who they are. From the deep truth they know.

Our daughters were so young at the time of the car crash that they do not remember any different reality than the one they know now. For them, I have always had a disproportionately large belly. I have always been challenged in the distances I can walk and in what I can eat. Because the car crash is a part of our family's narrative, they know in their mind that this was not always the case, but they do not have any conscious memories of things being different. In our basic daily routine while I recovered, I was not able to be anything I was not. It was not easy explaining why I could not pick them up. Why I could not sit by the dining table and why I would get up five minutes into a meal and go to rest. Why I could not play with them on the carpet or take them to daycare.

Naturally, though we faced challenges all along, the first few weeks and months were more intense. This was especially true immediately after the car crash, when the adults in the family faced enormous uncertainty themselves. Not knowing what to say resulted in saying nothing and trying to keep a regular routine when nothing in our lives was normal. For the twins, babies, not speaking themselves, would words have helped? Would it have been easier for them if something was more clearly said? I was not there. I cannot know for sure. Still, based on what I learned along my journey, and based on many mothers in challenging situations I have met since my own shattering, I strongly feel that acknowledging my absence with direct, honest words could have possibly calmed my daughters, young as they were. It is not the exact words that would have mattered, but the subtext within them, acknowledging that they too were going through something challenging and stressful. Having the adults around them reflect through themselves, saying, "Yes, this is hard," instead of making themselves act as if nothing is wrong. Children know when we are honest and when we hide information from them. They know even when we hide it from ourselves.

I do not recall my daughters asking a lot of questions until much later. Maybe it is because we shared. They knew why I needed to go for my operations and why things were the way they were because, after my return home, we often talked about it and prepared them. Children a little older than mine did ask many questions. They wanted to know how it happened, what happened to my car, and more. Once, about two months after I was back home, a curious five-year-old approached me. He just stared at me. Looking with his huge, deep eyes at the giant boot on my foot and my walking stick. Then he continued to look all over my body, the cast on my arm, the healing wounds still visible on my face and neck, the yet-to-be scars. He was fascinated.

"Does it hurt?" he eventually asked, bringing his big eyes straight to mine.

His father immediately tried to hush him, whispering to his boy that "It's not polite," looking at me apologetically.

I responded with an accepting look to the father – his intentions were good – and surprised myself by looking back directly into the boy's eyes, saying, "Yes, it hurts. Very much, but the pain is also becoming slightly weaker with time." I added with a smile, "It is not fun, but here I am, and you see, with my walking stick, I can manage to walk a few steps." Both parts of my answer were true, and that curious boy had a chance to meet wholeness weaved into imperfection.

Walking truth should be part of our daily existence. Like the trust we have that the sun will rise in the morning. We often claim we are walking truth, but we are not. In our demanding lives, we are so used to cutting corners and taking shortcuts, often not knowing anymore what is true and what is not. I have certainly used these tactics many times before. It is much easier not to deal with a disappointed friend who wanted to come over but cannot. This is especially true if it is our child we are trying to protect from that same disappointment. It is much easier to give some general excuse when we would rather keep some distance from someone than share with them how we feel. Unless walking very consciously, most of us in this fast-paced world face such moments daily. They become our "truth" and take us another tiny step away from ourselves. Truth, whole truth, that which comes from the knowing of our hearts, is often something we do not want to acknowledge. It so often does not fit the perceived literal reality we created for ourselves, so we specialize in ignoring it.

I think of myself before the car crash, and the truth that I was not on my path was there for a long time. Years. As soon as I started my master's degree, the message started coming through my body, as I was unable to deal with the stress of the academic environment. It got worse when I did my Ph.D. By the time I was doing my postdoc, the academic environment I was working in was so extreme in its demands that it was clear to me I did not want to live my life that way. I found myself working mostly from home, staying away from the office. During those years, I was continuously searching in my mind for other professional directions I could explore. I never made any real steps in those directions. But the understanding that my work was not aligned with me – and the discomforts associated with that – were there. The invitation to step forward toward who I was also came through energetic messages, intuitions, dreams, and visions I did not know how to relate to. I was afraid to listen to them. And as no clear path opened, I continued until the "boom" of the car crash and the LOVE of the NDE.

The fire of truth, inner and pure, clear and flawless, is our children's soul's essence, burning within. I remember it burning within me as a young child. Flames of knowing. Of confidence. Of joy. Pure joy. They were flickering, dancing, sometimes roaring and crackling louder. That is until I perceived messages that my fire should be reduced, hidden. It became so small that only a few embers remained hidden within me, waiting for an opportunity to reignite. When the fire of truth, of our being, is lit, burning, and present, it brings healing. The old, dry wood – the past issues that our children brought to resolve in this lifetime – are consumed. The density that enters their bodies when they are exposed to noise, pollution, extremism, or ignorance is consumed by it too and transforms into beautiful, deep colors of orange. Their proud and glowing fire brings balance to everyday encounters, to those incidents in which a small gap opens between the literal, physical reality and that of their hearts' deep truth. As long as our child's inner flame is burning and strong, it is a guiding force that helps them stay true to their being, to their essence. It is when the flames die down – often because we, their parents, their guides here in this dense world of ours, feed their fire with inappropriate food – that the gaps between the layers of our perceived reality introduce doubt to their beings.

In many cultures, even when there is abundance, the need to survive is so deeply rooted, inherited from generation to generation. And thus, when children face unkindness and cynicism, when they face lies, when they face violence and much more, even when our hearts go out to them, we very quickly refer to these incidents as hardening, as toughening, as strengthening, as necessary for their ability to cope in this world. "What does not kill you makes you stronger." Does it? It is pushing our children to close their hearts. It is putting out their inner fire, their soul's fire. And when we allow this, we distance them from themselves. Sadly, it enforces the same heritage that no longer serves our journey. This is a legacy many of us inherited from earlier generations. Some personal events are unavoidable, merely because the soul wants to resolve something. But almost every issue a soul brings with it can be solved in so many ways. When we walk truth, resolution comes easier, sparing us from undergoing severe trauma for it to happen.

When our children are born into this world, they do not speak English or Spanish, Hebrew or Arabic, Amharic, Japanese, French, Swahili, Chinese, Persian, Hindu, Russian, Quechua, Sign Language or any other language they later learn from us, those already on Earth, who are assimilated into specific cultural backgrounds. When they are born, when they come to us, they all speak one language, the same language, the language of the heart. And the heart knows only truth. If we are to love them, it is with our hearts. If we are to love them, it is about letting their hearts beat. Beat in the rhythm they know. Beat in the rhythm of their essence. Beat in the rhythm of truth. We can do that only if our own hearts beat truth. If our lips speak truth. If our mind thinks truth, and we walk our talk. It is easy to see why we forget. But this gives the excuses way too much room. We promised to LOVE. That is, to create the conditions our children need to be themselves. To stay true to their essence and the aims of their journey. It is about our promise to them to guide their lives here on Earth in a way that will not only teach them how to survive here but also guide them to stay true to themselves. To walk truth. To keep their hearts beating their essence.

Living truth starts with ourselves. It is about walking through life with awareness. It is about a conscious decision to listen to our hearts. To recognize our own power to know our truth and know that we are worthy of walking it. It is about making small daily choices based on the knowledge of our hearts. Choices that are right for us. Not because our mind, a creative manipulator, says some food is healthy, or that going out will make us feel good. But because we listen to the truth our body communicates to us. To the truth our heart knows. We all know what is true and what is not. We know this at all layers of our being. All we need to do is give this truth priority, turning it into the leading power in all our choices and daily moments. And when it comes to our children, who are born speaking truth, we must give them our example and reinforce what they already know. Let them keep the language of their truth, their native one.

What Is Your Truth? A Journaling Exercise

Truth is a complex concept, yet it is vital for our walk in life. This exercise offers an opportunity to expand your self-awareness of the layers of truth within you. Sometimes, our biggest shadow is our unwillingness to see. Once we see, many elements of life are no longer frightening.

Preparations: Take out a notebook or a blank piece of paper and a pen or pencil. Approach this exercise when you have at least 15 minutes, as usually it takes us a few minutes to gather ourselves, center, and put daily concerns to the side. If you would like to, light a candle, or prepare other ceremonial elements around you.

Starting: Close your eyes and take a few deep breaths. Feel your body relax, open your eyes and start writing. Write intuitively. Don't look back at what you write. You can write fluently or in lists of words. You can also sketch or draw your reflections on each prompt. I recommend responding to the prompts in order.

Prompts:

1. These are the actions within my day that make me happy...

2. These are the daily actions that do not make me happy...

3. When I act according to my heart's knowing, I feel...

4. I am walking truth when I am....

5. I am not walking truth when I am...

6. Today I was an example of walking truth to my child when I...

7. When I was a child, _____ and _____, and _____ filled me with joy.

Joy, deep and whole, is for many a sign of walking a moment of truth.

Attentiveness

MANY YEARS AGO, THERE was a young shepherd. He lived with his extended family in an oasis in the desert, with trees, birds, and a spring of pure, fresh water. Every morning he awakened to the first light, and started his days by blessing everyone. His days were full of beauty, yet his heart was unsettled. He waited. Mostly not even knowing he was waiting or why. Sometimes, his days were so full that he forgot. At other times, he was restless.

One night, he had a dream. And in his dream, he went on a journey, leaving everything behind. He woke up full of fear of what if and what will be. Yet, the thought of the journey was already stirring within him. And once it appeared within him, it started appearing within his family, until one day his father *said to him, "Go. Go. I will surely miss you, yet I know your heart is in need of motion, as my heart feels your need too."*

The shepherd packed his belongings. His brother packed his too, as he also longed for a journey. They kissed and hugged their family and started walking into the endless yellow desert. They walked and walked. The trail was challenging and not easy. Every step they took, something changed. Still, they walked lightly and full of joy. They walked their path. Then, after many days, they reached a crossroads. One road going down into the valley and to the city below. The other going up into the mountains. One brother knowing he must go down to the city. The other knowing he must go up the mountains. Neither could move, and they slept by the crossroads for days. Until one night, the shepherd dreamed again. And so did his brother. And when the sun woke up, lighting the world for a new day, they both knew that each of them has his way. They separated with love and continued on their ways. One down to the valley. One up to the mountains. Only they knew if they ever met again.

Being attentive. Being able to stop and listen within. Reaching out from within to hear all you need is the second universal element of our promise of LOVE to our children. One cannot be himself or herself without being attentive to their true authentic nature. Attentiveness starts with a breath. If we do not stop, even for a second, we cannot direct our attention. Without breath, conscious breath, the window to our awareness and ourselves is shut.

Only when you breathe can you start remembering the signs and directions you established for your own scavenger hunt. A game you hoped to joyfully play until your last years, finding many treasures you have hidden from yourself along the way, up until the last one to be found when your soul says farewell to your current body and returns home. Only when our children breathe can they listen to the truth they know and see the signs and directions they set up for their own game.

Attentiveness starts with breath. It is within our ability to notice our life's signs. Signs inviting us to eat, to rest, to exercise. Signs inviting us to explore something new, go on a trip, change a trip, cancel a trip, or decide to walk, drive, sail, or fly. Signs explicitly or indirectly helping us be at a specific time and place where we will run into another soul. Our best friend, our next work opportunity, possibly our future love and partner in parenting our children. Signs helping us know what to say or recognize what is true to us. Signs helping us notice what we need to see. Our authentic truth.

Imagine driving in an area you have never been to before. Not many others around. Every kilometer or mile looks the same. There are turns you can take and some roundabouts. All resemble one another. So you drive. You make an occasional turn, frequently wondering, "Have I been here before?" You look around, puzzled. So you turn to others to get directions. Some of them have internalized the social signs and are surprised you cannot see what everyone else sees so clearly. They tell you, "Is it not clear you should take that right lane to success?" or "You are thirty. You must take that second left and start a family." Others can see different signs, their signs, and may direct you to their destination, saying, "After you finish college, I think it is best to take the first exit in the roundabout directly to graduate school." And a rare few might recognize that maybe the signs they read are not the ones you read or are looking for, and they may suggest that "What is right for me is not necessarily right for you. See the nice park over there on the right? It is a good place to stop for a picnic and talk with your heart. It will give you the directions you need."

If you cannot read your signs, you follow whatever advice you manage to get. Including advice on how to parent your own children who chose you, and trust you, to be the parent they need. If our children cannot read their signs, they too will look for the help of others, instead of finding it within themselves, where it sits and waits. Their own inner wisdom. Most likely, especially when young, they will approach us, their parents, for guidance. Often, they will do this without words, simply by imitating our behaviors. Will we know what signs they need to follow? At first, following the advice of others gives a sense of control. "Oh, yes. Now I know where I am going." After some time, one gets lost again, looking around to see if someone else who understands the signs might pass by.

The thing is, no two people see, read, or need the same signs. No two children need exactly the same parenting, not even identical twins. Not when it relates to their unique personal path. So the only way to know you are where you should be, even if it is a deserted place in the middle of nowhere, is for you to be able to recognize and see your signs. Signs you had chosen, arranged, and posted before coming to your journey on Earth.

The signs we posted for ourselves come in numerous forms, ranging from an inner feeling to a sense of deja vu, or even something that your partner said. The signs and notes we hid from ourselves may also come in a confirming song we hear on the radio on our way somewhere, a person we meet at the grocery store, a butterfly flying around us, or a book enchantingly grabbing our attention at the exact time in life we need it, even if it is after it was sitting on our shelf unread for years.

Just as our children are born fluent in the language of truth, so are we, their parents. All of us are also born with the gift of recognizing our signs. However, somewhere along our journey here on Earth, many of us find that we cannot identify them anymore. Or worse, not only do we not recognize our signs, but we also stop having any access to them, developing doubt in their reliability. We trust others just because they wrote a book, or we completely forget our signs ever existed. Not trusting our own signs means not trusting ourselves. Not recognizing them means we do not have a true perception of who we are. When we cannot trust ourselves or know ourselves, life is full of unnecessary challenges. When our children cannot trust or know themselves, their life becomes full of unnecessary challenges. Is this what we want for them?

Would it not be easier if we could hear ourselves? Would we not be much warmer within if we were connected to the most significant person in our lives? Ourselves. When we are attuned to who we are, attentive to our being, we can see the signs for our path. Moreover, we can recognize them and follow them, having life become simpler, flowing, and joyful. And when we are attuned to our signs, to who we are, it becomes much easier for our children to be attuned to theirs because they are learning from, or imitating, an adult who is true to her path.

Attentiveness begins with a breath.

Within each breath, we have a small particle of time to read our signs for that specific moment. The little physical tingling we might feel. A hunger developing in our stomach. Is it heaviness or a sensation of joy lifting us? A wish to escape or excitement? A need to sit down or jump? A clear irrational "yes" or an urge to get out of a place as soon as possible? Clarity or discomfort stemming from a clash between our rational reasoning and that of our hearts? Reading our signs starts with our connection to our physical body and our emotions. It is about listening to our heart, soul, and essence, talking to us through our body, sensations, and feelings. If, at an unexpected moment, our body tells us it is tired and needs rest, maybe we should check whether we have done something incongruent with our journey, leading our body to hint that we should stop for a moment, rest, and by resting, create time to listen within. Maybe we have committed ourselves to participate in something that is not right for us, and our tired body invites us to consider changing that plan. Our body communicates with us at every moment, directing us to what we know, deep within. When we do not listen to it, it has no choice but to shout. A while ago, I signed up for an online course and looked forward to it. Then, as soon as the program started, my nose started running. There was no way I could participate in the class in that state. I carved through the first day. By the second, it was clear I was not continuing. The message, given through my body, was clear, and as soon as I was willing to listen to it, my nose immediately stopped running.

When meeting other parents who have experienced a shout from their body while coping with an illness, disability, divorce, being fired, or recovering from a car crash, as I have, what they all share is that the shout made them stop. At first, just stop. Not even realizing this is what's taking place. Busy with trying to understand what's going on and take care of the physical, literal situation. Then, they recognize they have stopped, and they start to observe and listen. To themselves and to their children. The newly earned ability to listen is most often accompanied by lots of noise from the doctors or from our family and friends who might know someone who experienced something similar. More than that, the noise derives from our internal representation of what we previously perceived as the way things are done, should be, or always were, all of which hinder our attentiveness. This makes us suddenly question all that we have previously accepted, without any deep consideration, as the way things are.

At the time of my healing, I got a lot of advice as to what I should be eating. Lots of meat and eggs, meaning lots of protein. No fibers or raw vegetables in any form. The recommendations did not fit with what I was learning about my body. But I was in a new situation, left with very short, still-healing intestines and an open stoma, and the doctors and dietitians were the experts. They knew which turn to take on the road to intestinal recovery. Indeed, some of their recommendations worked well for the initial stages of my recovery. I especially enjoyed one piece of advice given to me by a gastroenterologist who, in response to me telling him that I could not digest any chicken or meat, and that I threw up after these protein boosts, said that a good source of protein would be meringue cookies made of sugar and lots of egg whites. He recommended that I eat a lot of them every day and even taught us how to make them at home. It worked for a short while until I realized how badly the sugar made me feel. The thing was, like with our signs, the only ones who can reliably know what is right for us is ourselves. The only way I could recover – and today, the only way I can keep my intestines, and as a result, maintain my whole health – was by listening to my body talking to me. So even if the doctors, dietitians, or a naturopath said it was good for me to eat something, when I found myself running to the toilet soon after, vomiting, or even feeling a little nausea or discomfort, it was my body telling me that this was not the nutrition it needed. This attentiveness to my body's cues serves more than my physical body. It keeps me more energetic and has cleared the brain fog I was walking with for years, allowing me to be much more connected to my essence.

Throughout my journey, being reborn physically and spiritually did not leave me with any choice but to be attentive to my path. It was a shout. A very loud one. Ignoring it would have meant it was better to be physically dead. I had no choice but to relearn the signs I myself had set for my own scavenger hunt. To be attentive. At every painful moment. At every sad, angry, or frustrating moment. To listen to the information coming from within and recall my signs, notice them, and react to them. I had to be attentive if I was to become who I wanted to be when I first came to this journey on Earth. I had to be attentive to justify, if only to myself, my miraculous survival. To connect to my essence and gifts, to write on my website and in this book about the things I learned. To be me. To be as close as I can to who I am in my essence.

Attentiveness begins with a breath.

I did not breathe before my car crash. I dismissed many signs in the shape of discomforts, challenges, and intuitions sent to me so that I would wake up. I was playing my life's scavenger hunt game like kids play. Even before they figure out the specific assignment of the first stop or get clear on the direction to the next location, some of them are already running forward in the expected course of the game. I was on an academic path, so that was where I walked. Or, more precisely, ran. The universe reached out its hand many times, but I dismissed the signs.

When I was lying on our purple couch, watching my daughters with others attending to them, I had time to breathe. Breathe and observe. Observe and learn my family. I had time to breathe and get to know them. Breathe slower and get to know me. Breathe even slower, and realize they chose to come to me as their parent and because of this, I have some role in their lives, even if I do not do any of the caretaking. Breathe deep and know that I love them, and that to love them means I want them to be them. Breathe wider, expanding, and internalize that for them to be themselves, they need to know their truth. They need to be able to read their signs so that they can follow their path. Breathe a new breath, and realize my signs are not necessarily identical to theirs.

Knowing our signs does not mean we know our children's signs. We do not read the same signs as our children do. They come with their own set of signs. Some of them, huge souls, come with signs that we are not even able to see or understand. Yes, some of the signs they come with might be related to us or may even be very similar to our own. They did decide to come to us in the first place. Our journeys are at least partially related. But our shared walk cannot be generalized to every sign and every crossroad in their lives, even when they are young and so dependent on us. So, how can we serve them? How can we purely love them? In terms of attentiveness, we must guide them to know how to listen within because if they do not know how to listen within, they will not hear their hearts and will not remember their signs. We must support them in their attentiveness. Not at the age of twenty-five after going through some crises, nor after a car crash. Have them recognize what they already know. As babies, as toddlers, in second grade and the fourth, during middle school and high school, and when they continue on their journey as adults. Guide them in the importance of attentiveness so that it will be a primary tool in their lives. So that they can always be attentive to who they are, to the signs their body gives them, to their own truth. Not ever forgetting, thus not even realizing that it is innate for them to listen, and know, and remember. Knowing exactly when they need to pause and picnic for some time, where they need to turn left or exit to the right, when they need to drive in the same direction as everyone around them, and when they need to drive in another.

So what happens? How is it that as we come to Earth, as babies, as children, we come here knowing everything we need to know, and with the maps for every direction we will need throughout our lives, and then later in life, we lose our way, needing directions from others instead of trusting our own knowledge? Instead of reading our own signs, whether they come as physical or emotional discomforts, a knowing, an intuition, a gut feeling, a person coming into our lives at a specific moment, or a symbol reappearing again and again to attract our attention? Do we forget it all? Do we repress those little hints and signs along our way? Do we ignore them?

Unknowingly, with no bad intentions, only very good ones, we introduce our children to doubt in their own knowing from their very first days on Earth. If I had listened to the doctors – well, to some of them – my amazing healthy twins would not be here. It was a high-risk pregnancy. They shared a placenta, and at first, the doctors thought that they also shared the amniotic sac. When some of the tests came back with ambiguous results, some doctors advised that the pregnancy should not be continued. I was lucky to have a clear feeling that it was all fine. I listened. I was also fortunate to have a supportive husband who trusted my intuition. But there was stress in this pregnancy again and again. Doctors would limit their own risk by giving the worst prognoses they had, and we would have to take a deep breath again and again and trust our inner irrational feelings. Many women are more attentive to themselves when pregnant. Could this possibly stem from the clarity and purity of those we carry? Having them come with a basis of deep attentiveness and deep knowing of their truth?

Following the womb, babies need to adjust to their life with us. It starts with fundamental functioning. They feel a sense of hunger. Some mothers respond and breastfeed according to their baby's demand, reinforcing what the baby knows. I have a sign of hunger, I am attentive to it, I recognize it and respond by crying and telling my mom I am hungry, and I get the food I need. I know I will have more when I need more, so I take only as much as I need. For others, the reinforcement is in the opposite direction. I am hungry, I am attentive to it, I recognize it and respond by crying and telling my mom I am hungry; she ignores me because she was told to feed every three hours, or because she is on the phone, or taking care of other children in the family, or because of some other justified reason, so my tiny unaware interpretation may go: "Am I hungry? Do my signs to her mean anything? Maybe the next time she feeds me, I should take as much as she has to keep me full longer?" Then, personal doubt starts building itself, teaching the newborn baby there is no use in being attentive, distancing her from her instinct. Should we go on? Our baby is tired. But it is not the right time for us to put him to sleep. Maybe because we would rather have him sleep only once a day so that he will sleep through the night. Perhaps we would rather have her sleep when her older sister comes home from school so that we can have time for her. Or with twins, it is so much easier if they eat at the same time and sleep at the same time. Initially, when my twins would wake up at night, I would wake up to each one, responding to her personal demands. That meant I did not sleep. So from time to time, whenever one woke up at night, my husband would bring me the other so that I could nurse them simultaneously and thus manage to get some sleep in between. However, that meant we were synchronizing their needs, not attending to each on her own. What is right? There are so many justified reasons for why we do what we do. Life in the modern world is challenging. The thing is, each diversion from the communication we are getting from our babies makes them question their own knowing. Casts doubt on whether being attentive to those things our body tells us has any meaning.

Older ages heighten the challenges to endorsing our children's attentiveness. Who do they want to play with? What activities do they prefer? If our child prefers being home, having only a few friends, do we support them? When our child prefers not to go to a friend's house, do we listen to their request, even if we know how disappointed their friend will be? When our child is lying and daydreaming, do we let them? Are we okay with our children doing nothing and gazing for a while? When our child is not sure of something, do we give them the answer? Do we try to guide them to their own? Do we guide them to stop, listen, and be attentive? Are we accepting of our child's choices of afterschool activities? Of their friends? Do we always try to have them be active in various aspects to advance them? To open opportunities? Do our children have any quiet time? Do we give them an example of turning inward ourselves?

In my journey, I have learned that to bring LOVE, to be LOVE, I must first set an example of being me so that my daughters could be them. I found that when I wait for them to be attentive to themselves, they are always right. It is far from having them do whatever they want. It is about having them know for themselves. It starts with how much they eat or what they prefer eating. It goes on to inviting their friends over only upon their request and inviting only those they wish to meet. It means accepting their wishes to go somewhere or stay at home, even if we think some activity would be enjoyable or would support them socially. It means having them have a core so that social pressures do not easily influence them. Is it always easy?

No. When they were younger, it was uncomfortable to repeatedly refuse an invitation from sweet girls from their class. Nor was it easy to observe the challenges brought by not adhering to the social expectations of others. It is gratifying, however, to see them grow into little women who know who they are, mostly staying true to themselves.

Our references for raising our children come from our own upbringing, our families and culture – global practices seeping into our perceptions. The correct way for each child is within them and within the specific dyadic relation of a particular parent with a specific child. There is always a reason for their choice of parents. Going by what others do is very helpful when we do not hold the tools ourselves, or when our children bring with them challenges that others are already experienced with. But the truth is only within our children, and we should always be attentive to the direction they bring, to their preferences, to their requests from us, and respect them. Self-reference and discern what advice is aligned with the signs we see and what takes us in the wrong direction within our shared journey. I realize it is nearly impossible to avoid life's quick pace, preventing us from being attentive and thus deviating in raising our children. Life is often so rapid that we do not listen to ourselves and have no idea what our truth is. So how can we wait for another to be attentive to themselves, to what is truly right for them at a specific moment?

Do we recognize becoming hungry? Not when we are already at the stage of having to have something immediately, enhancing the chance of eating something we already know will make us feel bad. Can our children recognize they are hungry and eat something healthy on time, or, while still dependent on us, remember to tell us soon enough? Do we listen to our body asking to slow down? To exercise? To go to sleep? To dance? Do our children know the signs and limits of their bodies and adhere to them? Do we leave a bad job or a job that does not make us happy? Can we recognize people who are not good for us and back away from them – or the opposite, identify those who we want as our friends? Can we recognize whether places and crowds are good for us? Do we respect our children when they tell us they do not want to go somewhere or when they tell us in words, or in other ways, that some people we may like do not make them feel comfortable? Are we attentive? Do we follow our signs? Do we guide our children to be attentive to what they know? To follow their signs?

Creating the conditions that will allow our children to be attentive starts with us. We cannot have them stop, listen within, hear the truth of their hearts, and act on it if we do not stop, listen, hear our own truth, respect ourselves, and act on it. There are no clear dos and don'ts. It is about awareness and respect. It is about going out into nature, appreciating the butterflies, the sound of the wind rushing through leaves, or the sound of waves, and turning inwards. The younger we start, the easier it is to have our children be attentive to themselves. Develop an ability they are already born with, instead of teaching them the self-distrust we walk with.

Attentiveness begins with a breath.

To be LOVE is to be who we are in our essence. To love our children, truly love them, is to create the conditions they need to be their essence, to stay one, to walk their path, to be able to read their signs. To be able to breathe into themselves, listen within, and simply know what only they can know for themselves. Their truth. The signs they posted for their own scavenger hunt in this lifetime. To have them breathe, slowly, deeply, and widely, and work with the knowledge of their heart. Our role as their parents is to make sure they never forget how to breathe. Those who breathe know who they are.

A Basic Breathing Exercise

This is the most basic exercise there is. It is also possibly the most important one. In our speedy and full days, attentiveness is reflected in our ability to choose. It is in those moments of stopping. Not for an extended meditation and not to be writing in our journal. A brief second of vast awareness brought to us by breath. Attentiveness, especially in the middle of the fullness of parenting, starts with a breath. Allow me to invite you to try a quick exercise, one that has become a habit for me and that I find myself doing numerous times each day.

Take a deep breath. Feel how you fill your lungs. With air. With light. Pause. Put the book aside for a few minutes, and just be.

Breathe

Inhale

Pause

Exhale (Try to let all the air out)

Be

Take another deep breath

Notice, within the exhale, that slight movement within. Almost unnoticed. That clearing of the thoughts or feelings keeping you from the necessary awareness of this specific moment in time, enabling a light breeze that brings freshness to your being.

Breathe
Inhale
Pause
Exhale
Be
Be

Repeat every moment in which the winds around pull you out of your center. While cooking, while driving, or while listening to your child's stories of their day.

The Motion of Love

*M*ANY YEARS AGO, FLOWING *in the river of time, there was a beach. And by this beach, which was not too large, not too small, hidden by rocks, lived a girl. Her hair, thick from the salt water, ran down her back. When she kneeled, her lengthy hair softly touched the sand. The girl's skin loved the warmth of the sun. Her eyes sparkled to the sparkle of the water. She sat on the beach. She sat and stared at the water. She sat and waited. She waited in the morning. She waited at noon. She waited when the evening came, and the sun started to set, coloring the horizon in vibrating purples, reds, and oranges.*

One morning, a rabbit living in the rocks came to join her. Waiting with her. Staring with her. Wondering what she was waiting for. "She must know," thought the rabbit, looking at her sparkling eyes. A singing bird and a large-winged bird, both living in a nearby tree, joined them, also curious. They waited.

One evening, a strong storm visited the beach. The wind became stronger and stronger, whistling its song of change. Water fell from the sky. The girl and her friends all ran to hide. The water came storming up and down the beach's shore. Erasing all traces in the sand. Breaking into the sand dunes. Completely changing their landscape.

In the morning, the wind calmed down, the sea peacefully rested, and the world became quiet. The girl came back to her waiting place on the beach. And there, at what she knew was her regular spot, although it had changed so much during the storm, was a shell. A large shell. A conch shell. And in it was life. The girl's hands wanted to touch and take the shell. The girl's heart knew she must help the shell get back to the water. She carefully tried to pick it up. But the shell asked to be put back in its place.

"I must get to the water on my own," said the shell.

The girl and her friends were all surprised. "But there is a huge sand dune blocking your way," exclaimed the rabbit.

Respecting the shell's wish, they did nothing but wet it. The rabbit stayed by it, keeping it company. The singing bird sang to it. The large-winged bird flew above, shading it. The girl took a small bucket, filled it with water, and drizzled it over the shell and onto the sand just in front of it. And the shell moved very slowly. Step by step. Sorting the grains of the sand. Often, drifting backward, down the dune. Setting back on its way, again and again. Sand grain by sand grain.

After many, many days, the shell reached the shore. And when it did, it took a deep breath from the beauty of the water and the new friends it had acquired on its way. It breathed in the water's sparkle and the splendor of the day and closed its eyes.

The girl and her friends asked, "Why are you not continuing into the water?"

The shell smiled at them. "My journey was the way back to the water. I am yours now." The girl sat next to the shell, patting it softly and hoping, with the fullness of her heart, that her friend would live. Hoping, with the fullness of her heart, that he would go back into the sea. Every morning, she found the shell slowly sinking into a deep sleep. Then, one morning, when she reached the beach, she saw the shell was empty. The sea had washed the life within it back into itself.

The shell stood empty exactly at the waiting spot of the girl. The waiting spot where she had sat for days. Waiting in the morning, noon, and evening. The waiting spot where the rabbit, singing bird, and large-winged bird waited with her. The place where they first met the shell after the great storm. The girl carefully picked it up, intuitively brought it to her lips, and blew. A beautiful, deep sound came out. Strong, clear, direct. A call left in the shell for its friends. A call inviting them, saying, "Come. Come. Join me. Set out on your journey."

Parenting is a quest. The most magnificent of life's journeys, which we embark on when our first baby turns us into a mother or father for the first time. A sacred moment of new life. A sacred moment of streaming love and joy. A moment in which we hold, in our hearts, the promise of giving them the world, becoming better people, and providing them with all their needs. Sadly, as part of life, it may also be a moment of being absent, a loss or sadness for many possible reasons.

Parenting invites us to evolve merely by the rapid changes of our children's natural growth and development. One day we change diapers, and the next, we run after them in the playground. Then, we see them grow, becoming little men and women with preferences, thoughts, and opinions. Before we realize it, they are independent young adults walking their sacred path. Hopefully, adults who were given the conditions to sprout and grow, staying true to their essence. We evolve sand grain by sand grain and continue to do so as partners in our shared soul walk, even when it seems they have grown, leaving our nest and claiming to need nothing from us any longer. When we take the invitation and opportunity our children bring with them, their rapid growth does not let us stay behind. And reciprocally, our motion invites them to grow as well.

Being in motion, taking responsibility for our own walk, evolution, and growth, as part of the reciprocal partnership with our children, is the third promise we all made to our children. Actively moving toward our own healing, in parallel to raising our children, and providing them with their needs, is a necessary condition for them to flourish in their sacred walk on Earth.

What does it mean to be in motion and take responsibility? It means owning patterns, even if we can see that they come from our family, and that our father walks with the same faulty pattern we are trying to heal in ourselves. It means seeing where our limitations come from but not expecting the other – our mother, our partner, or our children – to do the work for us. It is looking in the mirror, as uncomfortable as it may be, and owning our whole selves. The positive characteristics and the gifts we walk with, together with the ones not serving us and inviting healing. We must walk in awareness, owning these traits and then doing what needs to be done to heal ourselves: our physical body, lifestyle, and nutrition, as well as our thought patterns, emotional or intergenerational traumas, binding perceptions, beliefs, and energetics. Thankfully, so many healing modalities are available today for us to work with.

Possibly, the healing of a wound carried down one of our ancestral lines, or the healing of intergenerational trauma, is something we set out to achieve as part of our journey in this lifetime – not only for ourselves but also for our families. Many children come with such a mission on their plate. Yet when we approach those wounds, determined to heal them, we do it first and foremost for ourselves, even if our children are the motivator for that healing. Any such healing can, and hopefully will, ripple down and up within our families. But the ripple depends on all those other souls in our families choosing to take in that healing. Some will, some won't. We can't know the path of another soul. The healing that worked for us could possibly serve other souls in our family. Alternatively, other souls may need to walk that healing path on their own, or in a different way than what served us.

Often, a crisis throws us into a whirlpool. When we manage to reach the water's surface and take a breath, we hopefully take it with an understanding that something must shift. When we reach the shore, a new one. We start by learning to breathe again, as only when we breathe can we be attentive. But what then? After the first, second, and third breaths of understanding, we are invited to a greater journey. To a deeper quest. How do we bring it into our lives?

For most days along my journey, it all felt so impossible that even taking the first step, that deep breath of a beginning, allowing a brief moment of attentiveness, saying yes to whatever would come, made me choke and freeze where I was. I needed a long, slow cooking time. Like a stew sitting on the stove, all its ingredients – vegetables, spices, and water – ready in the pot. The fire beneath it very low, yet never going out, its blended smell slowly coming out of the pot, reaching all around, starting to invite, yet needing more time, until it would be ready. While I was not aware of it, struggling to mentally make sense of everything that was going on, I had already said YES to the slow cooking. Multiple YES's. My heart said YES. So did my soul and my awareness. I said YES within my NDE, when floating back to my body. I said YES in my invitation to my friends, in the mother circle to share what motherhood means for each, without knowing I was setting the aim of my quest. I said YES in that unaware prayer, in those surprising words, expressed four days before the crash: "I want to be their mother."

Different from most children who speak the language of truth and are attentive within, we as parents must walk with a very intentional awareness, making a constant mindful effort to overcome the enormous, confusing noise around us. An effort to be attentive. An attempt to walk our truth. Consciously being mindful. And if we lose our way at some point, it is a path of sinking in the sand and moving forward very slowly. A path of falling many times along the sturdy roads but always getting up and trying again. Trying to be attentive. Trying to speak only the language of truth. For me, at first, it was more of a quest than a constant reality. A slow motion. A motion from moment to moment. Not even from event to event or from day to day. An intentional attentive motion, in which I tried to make my participation in life an aware one.

I found myself starting by sorting the sand grains of my life, the sand grains of my home. My search for a deeper meaning of what LOVE was and of how to bring to my daughters the divine sense of LOVE, acceptance, and joy I felt in my NDE led me to tiny soul moments: specific, distinctive, individual, short moments of alignment. Moments in which the layers of my existence came together, with all my parts connecting, guiding me to walk the deep truth of my soul. My unique way of walking my path in my personal motion.

These soul moments were not necessarily moments of awakening. They were not moments I would later remember. In line with my suggested definition of spiritually aware parenting as the *act of guidance and care for souls arriving on Mother Earth, creating the conditions for each soul to grow its physical vessel and spiritual conduit so that it can walk the path it asked for, manifesting its soul's journey*, our aim in our journey here is to walk our path here on Earth. This means that soul moments can be profound moments of awakening or deep knowing. Yet, as with our intention to create the conditions our children need to walk their path here on Earth, in their now, we more frequently experience soul moments in the very literal daily aspects of our lives.

For me, soul moments were and are moments in which my specific thought, feeling, or action at that distinct moment were the right thought to think, the right words to use, or the right action to perform. It was whether I said something out loud or kept a thought to myself so that another could finish saying what they had on their mind or just think quietly. It was whether I stayed in the living room or left it. A distinct moment of action – staying or leaving. Do I do as the doctors suggest, or do I trust what I hear my body telling me? As moments, specific and distinct, they can be about standing in front of the closet and deciding which color shirt to wear, determining whether to answer a text message immediately or when we are not with our children, or choosing whether to say yes to that extra cube of chocolate we desperately wish for.

In their depth, each such soul moment is a moment of our various, physical human layers, emotions, thoughts, and actions being aligned to the journey our soul asked to walk. These are moments in which we are connected to ourselves, to who we are in our essence. These can be moments of alignment or moments when we may notice a lack of alignment in our automatic reaction or thought pattern and, in awareness, invite ourselves to feel, think, or act in a way more aligned with our inner knowing. Sometimes we walk aware of our soul knowing. At other times, we won't be able to put it into words, but we will still have the option of acting according to our inner guidance. Our soul's knowing is always present. Often, the challenge is our willingness to listen to it and trust ourselves.

As I healed, every soul moment I experienced was a grain of sand that would potentially be part of a brick. A brick that potentially would be part of a pillar. A tiny step towards the creation of a bridge. A bridge of knots connecting my human physical experience with that of heavenly LOVE. Integrating my physical reorganization and all that I came back with from my NDE, which I have reinforced in my journeying. Often, the bricks would not hold. I needed to start over again and again, learning the right combination of my sand grains and the water they need. What type of dry material to add? Finding I must allow the bricks the proper frame and drying time. Patience and serenity. Then, I started knotting the bridge itself. Sometimes it was a little insight that enabled the right knot on the bridge's connecting rope. Sometimes, the ties I made were either too tight or too loose, inviting adjustments.

Each brick and each knot were created in many separate and short moments. Distinct moments in which I tried to be aware of and walk in congruence to what my heart was inviting me to think, feel, do, say, eat, or be. Moments in which I could both be attentive to my deep core, to who I am, and speak through the language of truth. About a month and a half after the crash, still in the hospital, when I was allowed to try eating, food was immediately a source of comfort, as it had never been in my life before. I had not been eating for weeks, so I was able to take only a few bites. But I wanted more. My mom, when getting herself some red lentil soup at one of the hospital's cafés, also bought an avocado sandwich for later. It was fresh. Crunchy whole bread. Full of vegetables. A perfect combination. I can still remember its smell and its flavors in my mouth. I enjoyed it and took that extra bite. Like clockwork, a few minutes after I would eat an extra bite, I vomited. Then, in the first weeks at home, exploring what I could digest and what I could not, what worked with the stoma and what worked less, I also learned that when eating the daily baby orange soup my mom made for me – a puree of carrots, sweet potatoes, and squash, no herbs or any additional flavors – I needed to be aware not to take that extra spoonful. That extra spoonful is what distinguishes a soul moment from an unaligned one. If I leave it in the bowl, I am attentive to my soul's knowing. If I take it in, I am not.

At first, I experienced very few soul moments, and I did not even realize when I was not attentive or aligned. Then I found I was able to spot those moments, which felt as if, for a brief second – one full breath – Earthly time stopped, and I was either attentive or truthful or both. Slowly, the frequency of such moments grew. First, in the very literal aspects of my life. I learned that as far as food goes, recognizing that extra, unwanted bite takes place before I feel full. It is a type of analysis, often an unaware one, of recognizing which bite will leave me happy and comfortable not in that second but an hour to two hours later. I learned to calculate what I can handle in each day and make choices. Spending time with my daughters was more important than spending it with others. Finding time for my journaling and, at first, for drifting to the light that helped me become calm, and then intentionally journeying to explore, broaden, and connect were elements that, once I chose them, also allowed better managing of my literal life. This opened an opportunity for more short Earthly time stops, aligned with where and how I wished to walk in my essence.

As soon as I started recognizing soul moments, the unaligned ones frustrated me. I understood. I understand. They are part of the never-ending learning process. A moment of walking away from the living room because I could not cope with the noise around me was often an unaligned moment, as my daughters did need my presence, even if it was a fairly absent one. Sometimes, the same act of walking away from the living room was precise because it freed those around from constantly watching over me. The choice to go back to teaching seemed like the right choice when I made it. Later, it was revealed as a step that was very inaccurate to my soul's yearning. Would I have managed to carve my way without this step of returning to academic teaching and finding I am unable to do it anymore, helping me close that door? I will never know. It was part of the trail I found myself taking, and all I can do now is be an observer of it, not judge what has been. Every day—morning, noon, afternoon, evening, and night—I choose. I choose to walk in awareness and attentiveness with the aim of accumulating soul moments. Moments in which the literal facts of my life, and the various layers of who I am, are aligned. And I forgive myself in the many moments when I do not.

So possibly, today, over ten years later, on a Monday morning, I manage to begin my day early, starting it with some slow breathing, a moment of "me time" with my journal, getting clear on my focus for that day, what I should be attentive to, what I should be attentive to in regard to each member of our family, including those walking on four legs. On Wednesday, I might not manage to get out of bed, drag myself out completely sleepy, and take deep breaths while trying to figure out what's going on around me, what needs of others must be attended to, and what can manage to happen without me. Luckily, the older my daughters get, the more they manage without me on such mornings. And in addition, I have a very supportive and involved husband on my team. Both days can continue as they started. The Monday example sets me on a day full of soul moments. Having clarity in the morning facilitates more precision throughout the day. The Wednesday morning example invites me to a very attentive day. Attentive to myself. Resting. Eating. An invitation starting at the literal, physical aspects, then broadening to the other layers of life. Both days can also flip. In the Monday example, although the chances for this happening are lowered as I start very focused and am thus attentive to that day's invitation, I might experience an inattentive moment because I may carry on with the noise of life, letting it in more than is healthy for me, and I will then need the Wednesday example to collect myself back into my core. A Wednesday morning may invite such an invitation to be attentive to myself. If I indeed listen to it, I will rest, possibly winning another wakeup, a new one, allowing for a new start for that day.

The dance of life is an aware one. To dance it, we must participate. We cannot partake if we stand by the ballroom walls, expecting another to invite us to dance. No one can dance my life for me. No one can dance my daughters' life for them. I, their mother, and my husband, their father, cannot dance for them either. We each, parents or children, must take our own unique dance steps and show up on the dance floor. Dancing our unique journey. We cannot dance for another. We can only dance with them. The dance of life and participation starts with living it with awareness. Awareness in which I repeatedly observe and ask myself: is this the aligned move or not? Am I walking a soul moment? It is being in continuous motion.

Our bodies talk to us, and our soul communicates through them. Our bodies are a tool for us to use, to know if we are aligned or not. They reflect whether a step is comfortable, whether it is smooth, whether it feels good, or whether it needs practice or gets completely stuck. Is it expanding and widening, is my heart opening, do I feel a tingle of whole joy, confirming the precision of the moment?

While we each must dance our own dance, we do not dance alone. My dance, each individual step I take, is not only about me. It affects the steps in the dances of my daughters, husband, and other close family members. The dance, our own steps, moves, and choices, is never solo. Being ourselves, our essence, takes place in congruence with those around us, as we are each connected to many other souls. It is like the stars. They are all connected by delicate golden threads. Almost unseen. In a complex way, tangled to the naïve eye. When one star lights up, at first, it starts to shine from within; then, its light starts shining to its outer layers, reaching those edges of the delicate ropes connecting it to other stars. When this happens, it sends an electric signal, not necessarily visible, to those stars it is connected to, sparkling and lighting other stars via reflection. And when these light themselves, they send their own signals to other stars they are connected to. Reaching much further than they ever knew was possible.

When all our layers are aligned to our essence, to our core, when we dance our dance even for only one distinct soul moment, when we are attentive to our inner invitations, listen to them and respond to them, owning our journey, the universe responds. When we are true to who we are, it reinforces our motion and supports our dance along our path. Confirming that a specific step is the right step, that it is on the path, that it is the right exit in the roundabout. When we learn our steps and start accumulating soul moments, we enter congruence with the universe. More than this, we send an invisible signal to those sharing our lives with us. A quiet, loving message sent to our children, partner, and often others, saying: "I am in the motion of LOVE," "I am trying to align the aspects of who I am," "I am choosing awareness. I am choosing me. I am owning and am taking responsibility for my healing, I am choosing my soul's path," giving legitimacy, quietly inviting our children to also enter their motion of soul moments. Walking the beauty that they are.

Children and parents reciprocally influence each other equally. When either one of our children, or we, the parents, experience a soul moment, the domino effect reaches us all and brings alignment to everyone. It is so, even if it may not seem so immediately. For example, the more I spend my time writing, the more I need to be writing. Writing and rewriting fill me with whole joy – a sign of alignment with one's essence. I know now that I must write, even if just for myself. There are more and more moments in which I need to stop what I am doing and go to my notebooks to jot down an idea or write something. If this is indeed what I should be doing, my daughters simply keep themselves busy, doing their things. I find myself writing quietly, often much longer than the few moments of just jotting something down. If my urge to go write something is not aligned, it must not be an idea worth keeping. Something more important might be going on, and I would miss it while trying to write. I would not manage to. My daughters would need me. They may fight. They may become hungry just as I sit down. They may bring a book to read by my legs. Trying in delicate or more explicit ways to point out that we are not aligned. It is about more than setting an example or aligning in our state of being. It is about a constant mutual reflection.

As we are all entwined, sharing the same woven fabric of our lives, the same is true when one of my daughters or my husband has soul moments. An awareness and choice related to their unique journey. If it is a soul moment for them, then it will align for all of us. Possibly beyond us. The mutual effect of alignment takes place in tiny, literal, seemingly insignificant occurrences in life, such as our choice of meals, the timing of daily activities, and whether we return a phone call now or in fifteen minutes. It also takes place in larger-scale decisions and events, such as a change of career or a family move to another country. Both tiny and large-scale occurrences are equally important. Sometimes it happens only within us, possibly without any awareness, but it is still the alignment of two or more souls walking together.

Without consciously being aware of it, we are always in search of soul moments. Children, still speaking truth, still being attentive to it, are especially drawn to these moments, as these moments reinforce what they already know. They can recognize others walking truth and being attentive from afar. In parallel, they easily identify the adults that do not. Each soul moment they witness in others gives them legitimacy to continue being themselves. Validating what they know. Giving them permission to be. The establishment of soul moments of accuracy and alignment is like nurturing a seed and its soil, covering the seed well, keeping it warm and moist. Providing the basic nutrition it needs. The nutrition promised as part of its existence.

Even if it may not seem as such, we all experience soul moments. It may only happen once a day, when we stop what we are doing and sit down, listening to our thirst and drinking some water, or when we ignore a message that just popped on our phone because we know it is not the time to respond. Once aware of them, we become more intentional about finding alignment and thus invite more soul moments. Our criteria for such moments are within. Once we become aware of the synchronicities, once we realize, "Oh, that was a soul moment," we are soon to recognize more such moments and the feelings that accompany them. Often, the clarity that such moments bring is so bright that it is impossible to ignore them, and we simply know. For me, such moments are often accompanied or followed by a sensation of whole joy. It is not happiness or cheerfulness. Nor is it bliss, enjoyment, or delight. It is more a sense of contentment. Of serenity. Of unity. It is a deep, peaceful feeling, knowing that, contrary to all that may seem to suggest differently, what is occurring is the most aligned thing in that particular moment. Feeling it in my body. And if it is indeed the most aligned for me, then it is such for those that I love: my daughters, my husband, our parents, and for the universe as a whole.

When we touch on soul moments, we know we are on our path. Knowing a specific step is or was on the path we wished to walk does not mean anything more. It is about that specific step. That specific moment in time. The specific soul moment. It does not hold any information about where our path will lead us. What is hiding after the next hill, after the third exit on the roundabout, or whether the next time we place our foot on the path, it will take us to where our hearts yearn to walk. It is about that moment only. When we recognize and accumulate soul moments, we are no longer trying to get, as fast as possible, to a defined destination, a defined destiny, or a defined mark as set by our social or cultural environment. We can just walk our path. Step by step. Soul moment by soul moment. Sand grain by sand grain. Focusing on staying on our trail by being attentive and adherent to our truth. Letting go of any need to control the outcome.

And in this dance of soul moves, like the communication of stars, we unknowingly create even further waves. Since around our very close family, that of our partner and children, there are many others. Our sisters and brothers and their families, our parents, our friends, and our children's friends. A wave of alignment always penetrates the light bodies and energy of others around us. Similar to the truth that babies bring into our lives. Most of us are unable to ignore them. Having them push a button most of us forgot ever existed. These waves of alignment tickle the truth in others. Awaken their inner quest for their own attentiveness. It triggers the wish to go inward. To touch oneself in the heart. And just the same, when others have soul moments, it triggers us, invites us, and the cycle of ripples grows.

To truly LOVE, you need to let another truly be. To let another truly be, you first must be truly you – your authentic self. On the path to becoming us, we create ripples and waves. Those ripples allow those around us to awaken to their truth as well. Not to our truth. To theirs. For most of us, it does not happen at once. It is always a process of collecting soul moments. Each moment is a new start of LOVE. A unique chance to be attentive and walk our truth. When that happens, a ripple is sent to our children. Letting them know we are in motion. This knowing is vast and valuable. It allows them to accept who they are. Helping them avoid the pitfalls modern society is so eager to pull them into. Every moment of attentiveness and truth we, their parents, have keeps them attentive and true to themselves. They create conditions for our children to remain themselves, increasing the chances that they will remain on their path. They will not be distracted by the noise of the world and will be able to focus on what they came here to do. To learn. To serve. To bring. They will be able to remain the LOVE that they are.

Communicating through the one language that unites us all – the language of truth – together with continued attentiveness and adherence to our signs and path sets us in motion toward a life of LOVE. A life of wholeness and joy. To LOVE our children is to create those conditions they need to remain themselves. It is avoiding all the obstacles tempting us to be someone else, as outlined by society's expectations. Guiding them to be who they are so that they too will be able to grow into adults living a life of wholeness and joy. The one way for this to happen within our family starts with us. We, parents, must first be ourselves. Take responsibility, own, and heal our wounds, embrace the light within each of us, and devote ourselves to the LOVE that we are, allowing our children to surf on the ripples we create. Creating an environment that will nourish what they know, who they are, so that they will not forget, as so many of us have throughout the years. We promised. We promised to love them. For me, that is what parent-child LOVE is about.

A Daily Question for Recognizing Soul Moments

Once we walk aware of our wish to bring more alignment into our days, the first step is to enhance our awareness.

Starting at this moment, ask, "Should I be reading this book now?" (Yes/No), "Is it right for me to bring attention to whether I am aligned or not?" or "Is _____ aligned for my child?"
Your answer might be yes. Your answer might be no. Both are fine. Just notice.

If you are unsure, see it as unaligned.

Ask this question of alignment about every little element of your day.

Start with just noticing. Most likely you will notice that, like most of us, you have more unaligned moments than soul moments. No judgment. After bringing our attention to the alignment of our day, merely recognizing that something is not aligned encourages us to avoid it or do what does feel aligned at that moment. Slowly, we walk more soul moments and dance in the motion towards our true path.

Only the Beginning

*O*NCE, THERE WAS A *tree. Its trunk is long and tall. Its roots reach deep into the earth. Its long branches and leaves reach high into the sky above.*

One day, a child walked by. He touched the bark and felt the tree's heart beating. He walked around it and admired its thickness.

"It must be very old," the child told his grandfather.

"Yes," his grandfather responded. "It is indeed." He looked at the tree and felt the delicate warmth of love simmer in his heart. "You know," he told his grandchild, "This tree has always been here. Long before we came to this land. I hope it will continue living here long after I am gone." He sighed. "Maybe one day,"

he added, winking, "maybe one day you will bring your new wife here, and then your children."

The child ignored him, bending down to look for a broken piece of wood he could carve.

They sat by the tree, and the seasons passed. Autumn winds came, and the leaves changed their colors and fell to the ground. Winter storms bedecked the tree in a beautiful white dress. Then, the white dress bent the old and weak branches with its weight, until they too fell to the ground. Late winter, blending with early spring, sparked a new beginning, new twigs, and first flowers. The tree woke from its winter hibernation, welcoming the birds and the awakening life around. When spring fully smiled, flowers blossomed with a sweet, delicate smell, and little fruits started to emerge.

Then it was summer. The tree was now clothed in a beautiful green dress. The child, now an adult, stood next to his beloved tree. He thought of his grandfather, and their many hours by the tree's trunk, laughing, touching the earth, carving toys from the fallen branches, sharing secrets and stories, often just sitting in silence, talking with the tree through their hearts.

"Let's walk around," he said to his daughter, reaching his hand out to hers. They tried to hug the trunk together, but it was wide.

"Maybe when your baby brother grows a little," he told her, "The three of us will hug it together." The tree smiled within.

Oh, then, the man lifted his daughter to his shoulders for her to reach the fruit. The tree bent its branches to bring them closer to her little hands. She took one, bit into it, the juice dripping over her mouth. So sweet. So delicious. Fresh and rich. She had never tasted fruit like this before.

"Do we have a bag?" she asked her dad. The man, respectful, asked the tree for permission. The tree, loving this man and his family, wholeheartedly agreed. It grows these fruits every year, hoping to share them with the world. Then the man handed the bag, waiting in his pocket, to his daughter, remembering the days he was on the shoulders of his grandfather.

"I'm filling it up for mom!" his daughter called excitedly, half mumbling with another fruit already in her mouth. "They are yummy."

They sat by the tree, enjoying the sweet, nurturing fruit. Smiling, the man thought that if as a father, he manages to guide his daughter in only this, to love this tree, to be connected to it and to others, as his grandfather taught him, it means he has given her the whole world. He looked at his daughter with grateful love. She looked back with the gratitude of bright light, with the knowledge of her heart. He is the father she chose for this lifetime. He loves this tree. He remembers.

More than ten years have passed since the car crash and the NDE. It is Thursday afternoon. My daughters are up in our open attic. They place a candle in the middle of the room. Then, they decorate around it with crystals. Today, one of them asked to create a spiral. All the colors of the rainbow are present.

"Mom, should I bring your drum up?" One of them asks. "Can we use mine today?" She adds.

And I, not always sure what we will need, reply, "Bring my drum, and all the other instruments, too. Don't forget your notebooks and the colored pencil box," I add, while mixing the red lentil soup already bubbling on the stove. "And turn the fan on," I tell them while turning off the fire below the quinoa pot. It's still full of water, but I know myself. If I leave it on, it will burn. Once the water boils, I let it cook itself. It is better not to trust my memory.

"I'm preparing the water and glasses," calls one of my daughters.

Another asks, "Where are the macadamias?" We always prepare macadamia nuts, as we find them great for grounding.

My third daughter quietly takes out some dates and puts them in a nice bowl on the table. Soon, a bunch of their friends and their moms will start walking in.

Our dogs bark. All four get excited, and this is our sign that someone has parked by our house. Within five minutes, our house is full. Friends of the girls, some with their younger sisters, together with their mothers, come for our weekly family shamanic journeying group. After exchanging hugs and engaging in short chats, we all go up to the attic. We each have our regular spots. Four moms, each with her daughters next to her.

"Who would like to light our candle today?" I invite one of the younger members with my eyes. I am filled with gratitude to see how she dawdles while bringing her intention into the candle lighting. Children know. All others are finding their comfortable spot, moving their bodies until everyone feels calm and relaxed.

"Let's close our eyes," I invite them. Some do, while some journey with their eyes open. We try to have as few rules as possible. Children know so much more than we do. "Take a deep breath...." I continue, and the drumming sound joins the rhythm of my voice.

Once upon a time, a tale of old begins. Once upon a time. Time. Tale. Story. Stories of life. What is the expected story? A tale of time? A tale of humans? A touching one? Will the ending be happy? Joyful? Surprising? Sad? And can we let go of the story and walk only with its gifts to us?

We all walk with stories, and as humans, we are all storytellers. Storytelling is shared among all cultures and all traditions of our diverse world. We share our stories in words, in art, in conversations and classes, in ceremonies, and, in our present phase of evolution, on social media. Moreover, we all share our life stories in the way we walk our lives and the wisdom we carry. And while I shared my story in this book, I also worked hard these past years to release the energy that it carried, hoping to walk its teachings and the many gifts it brought without getting stuck in its narrative. I also hope that this is what you will walk with after reading: the awareness, the truth, the attentiveness, and the motion – the gifts.

My story starts, continues, and begins again with enormous gratitude. Heartfelt, eternal, and profound. Joyful and bright. Gratitude that, just like LOVE, bubbles into every cell of the body. My body. I was given a chance for life. And even if at first, my attempts focused on coming back to the life I had before, it was not what the invitation brought by the crash was about. Eventually, I understood. Yes, sometimes it takes time. But when I realized it, I turned to focus on creation. The creation of my life. Full participation. Conscious and aware. Taking responsibility and owning. An ongoing process. Many new beginnings. Almost every day. Creating me as the person I wish to be, here and now. Creating me as a mother. The mother I promised to be when emerging back into life as a baby myself. The mother my daughters chose.

Creation. Creating. In retrospect, I guess that in the first part of my life, I related to these terms in two, somewhat (actually, very) limited ways. The first was related to old texts—namely, the Jewish tradition that surrounded me, although my home was secular. And the acceptance of other people's authority, limiting what is allowed, communicating what is right, decreasing one's ability to create and walk by the guidance of their heart. The second was my perception of the world of creative humans. I believed that creation, and creating, takes place only in the spheres of the arts, in crafting a painting, a sculpture, a song, or a performance.

As a child, I would spend hours with my mother and grand-ma, sewing, knitting, and making sculptures from newspa-pers mixed in flour and water. My brother and I would rip old newspapers into pieces of various sizes. Our hands turned black from the ink, and my mother would ensure that we stayed by the kitchen table. While we were ripping up the newspapers, she would prepare a mix of white flour and water. Then, we would start dipping pieces of the newspaper in the flour glue and create. I did not understand then that every-thing is creation.

My grandma was a creator. As I grew, we made many things together. My favorite was sewing dolls with her. For my twins' first birthday, a month before the car crash took place, I wanted to sew three dolls, one for each of my daughters. When I was a child, there were hardly any instruction books. My grandma taught me what her grandmother had taught her. Now, there are numerous resources. Yet, with all the instructions I had at hand, I encountered some challenges. My beloved grandma, then already over ninety, with advanced dementia, came for a playful afternoon visit around our little ones. While she sat on our purple couch, I tried to show her where I was stuck, hop-ing for guidance. She looked at me, and without any words, she took the head of the doll I was holding, asked for a needle, and started working. I was a little hesitant. I'd worked on that doll head a lot. But then again, the doll-making was in her hands. So while she could not explain, her hands remembered. I often feel that the memory held in her hands is like the memory of being more than a physical body, the memory of our energy, of the LOVE we all are. Finding it challenging to put it into words but walking it daily.

While there was no real rush, I wished to finish the dolls for the twins' first birthday, and I did. The thought of putting a loving note from me within their stuffed bodies repeatedly visited me. It was a key feature in one of my favorite childhood books, where the mom and daughter find each other after many years apart because of a note the mother placed within the body of a stuffed bear she sends her daughter as a present. Eventually, I decided that I wouldn't. Sometimes, I wonder if I thought about adding these notes because somewhere within me, I knew I might not be there for long. And then, did I choose not to add those notes because I also knew I would become their mother again? It was only a month after their first birthday that everything turned around.

Reflecting, my heart warms to these graceful memories, touching on an ever-existing idea – one that, like many others, I had to experience myself to capture its whole meaning. Life is about creation, and creation is not limited to any specific domain. I am a creator. It is in my every day. I do not prepare a meal; I create it. My day does not control me, crafting its appearance; it is I who make choices about what I do, the order of things, who I spend time with, and in what ways. Sometimes, I create it merely by choosing how to address those elements that might seem out of my control or accepting there are many things I do not know.

When I was recovering, the real healing could only begin once I let go of trying to be who I was before the car crash. Once I realized that a crisis, like an earthquake, does not come to shake us and have things return to the way they were. Like an earthquake, crises occur because there is an unseen pressure somewhere, needing a resolution. And the resolution is always a new configuration of the Earth. A new configuration of us. Either in the deep layers, unseen to us, or on the outer layers, with a felt shattering of our life. The only choice left was whether to participate or not. A choice between withdrawing from life, as I did in all those moments of distancing myself, of hiding under my covers, and justifying my absenteeism as the right decision – or a choice to participate in the creation. The creation of me. The creation of me as a mother. The creation of my family. The creation of all aspects of life. The creation of this book.

Four days before the car crash, in that circle of mothers and babies, in our old house, I unknowingly sent a prayer into the delicate net of LOVE we are all part of. "I want to be their mother" were my exact words. I prayed to stay here on Earth with my three daughters. Little did I know the journey my family and I were to embark on. In a prolonged and continuous process, I learned what my parenting can be about. At first, it didn't include any caretaking, any touch; it was as if I were a picture frame on the family's wall. This slow process invited me to listen and internalize the broader possibilities hidden within the essence of the parent/child soul relationship and its sacred nature. To realize and understand that my daughters had chosen me. That I had also chosen my parents. Your children chose you, and likewise, you chose your parents. And being chosen by a soul as its parent has commitments that we also agreed to, merely by coming to Earth ourselves, and in our choice of human parents, we expected precisely the same things. The journey took me to a place of awareness of those aspects that, even when I was unable to do any of the caretaking, still made me my daughters' mother.

Stories meet each of us where we are. My narrative, and the details I find myself sharing, changes as I tell my story to different listeners. When I was still in the hospital, a friend of mine looked for books that would relate to my situation. Neither of us understood at that point how big the shattering in our life was. She found some books sharing inspirational stories of similar crises and amazing personal rehabilitation and healing. I managed to start reading most of them only about a year after the car crash and the NDE. For a long time, I was unable to hold a book, and my attention span was extremely short. Even when I started reading them, I would enjoy the reading, but then, a few minutes later, I would have no idea what I'd just read.

Among these books, there was one that greatly influenced the narrative I choose to share with you. That book avoided the one aspect that was burning within me. The author didn't write about her child. Where was he now? How had their relationship been affected? How does she mother him today? He was present in her story, but very much in the background, even though he was the motivation for her healing. I, dealing with being absent, wished to know more about her parenting. It led me to seek answers. I needed to find something that would apply to what I was going through in my absentee parenting. I desperately needed parental guidance from other parents. Over the years, I found more and more, but I didn't find the book I really needed – the one that also related to the spiritual (beyond religion) nature of parenting, which had opened to me in my journey. Eventually, I wrote one.

When the writing in my journals started to invite me to write for more people than myself, I knew I wanted to reflect on parenting. Writing about my parenting was not trivial. It is one thing for me, as an individual, to choose to share my journey with others. However, as we are all connected, it is an entirely different issue when exposing others – in this case, my daughters, my husband, and my parents – in such sharing. Their story is not mine to tell. The writing process was a delicate dance between elements my story could not go without and elements that needed to stay out of it; I decided to leave out related stories from our lives, for the sake of preserving my family's privacy. Eventually, I feel that the process of putting it all together, the creation of this book, a magical entity of its own, took me – and takes us all – far beyond my family's specific examples and sharing. It also carries us beyond the experiences of families dealing with any crisis, allowing a glimpse into the universal aspects at the basis of any parent/child relationship.

We all want our children to be happy. Content. Joyful. We all want our children to dance their journey and sing their songs. Yet, we often forget that they are not *ours*. They do not belong to us. They have their path, gifts, and service to walk. We have been gifted with walking a sacred moment with them. We are partners on the journey. Both of us are simultaneously teachers and students for one another. Our seemingly human maturity and age place us, as parents, in the position of guide. But we must very delicately provide this guidance. Walk beside them and avoid taking the role of the teacher. The most aware and authentic way for us to provide this guidance is to walk who we are. Clear. Pure. Love.

Many of us, as an inherited form of parenting, sacrifice our own happiness for our children's future. I assume that by this point in the book, it is clear that our happiness is not mutually exclusive. Deep joy, that which bursts out from our essence, core, and soul, is there only when we adhere to who we are. Our children can find their own way and fight to be them-selves, as so many of us, now parents, had to do. Alternatively, their journey can be much easier if they have us to look to. When we permit ourselves to be who we are, we allow them to be who they are. For me, this is the only way to be genuinely joyful. To live the abundance of the light and the LOVE we are, here on Earth. Creating the conditions my daughters need to walk this way is how I share with them the pure, vibrating, accepting LOVE I experienced in my NDE.

Our children, when they arrive, know it all. For them, it is not about remembering, as it is for us, the adults, the parents. We are the ones who have been living here for a while, betrayed by the noise around us and by survival mechanisms that are often less relevant than they were for earlier generations. Our children know. They speak the language of truth, so crucial for them to stay on their path. They are one with the Earth and its elements. They are one with the universe. They are one with themselves. As part of our promise of LOVE, we promised to guide them in keeping this language of truth alive – beating, pulsing, gushing, and flowing as a natural part of their rhythm. It is our commitment to them to keep this fire of truth alive, burning, growing, leaping, and thriving.

Thus, we must know our truth, whispered to us by our hearts. We must help our children to know their truth, whispered to them by their hearts. For this to happen, attentiveness must be an active tool. We must preserve our children's ability to be one with everything around them. Different children and different parents have different ways of listening within – meditation, active mindfulness, walking, jogging, swimming, dancing, music, painting, knitting, sewing, wood carving, going out into nature, drumming, repeated movements, active dreaming, journeying with closed eyes or open eyes, and so forth. We each must find the way that best allows us this crucial attentiveness to our own truth. We must make ourselves time to breathe, as attentiveness starts with a breath. As parents, it is our responsibility to set both an example of such attentiveness and support our children in preserving their innate ability by not interrupting them when they go inside or when they connect with nature. We must support their choices and the truth they bring forth. And when needed, we can offer various tools and alternatives for being attentive, enabling them to weave their truth with that of life's literal reality, bridging the gaps with respect, and not taking away their power or dismissing what they know.

If we as adults, as parents, are yet to be clear about our truth, and if we are still working on cultivating deep personal attentiveness, this does not mean our efforts are insignificant. Our children come with an alert set of sensors, especially when it relates to us, their parents. Every tiny, unseen step a parent takes to work on their attentiveness recaptures the language of truth within their children. Every moment a parent is attentive to their own signs sends children the signals they profoundly need, assuring them that the language of truth they know so well is indeed the right one. Such moments invisibly confirm that the signs our children get for themselves are indeed truth. So, even if we are just taking our first steps, the mere motion on our behalf feeds that of our children. Hence, it invites us all to dance as a whole, each moment led by another member of the family, children and parents alike, creating our unique family dance.

We get into the motion of LOVE by accumulating soul moments. Moments in which we breathe, are attentive, recognize the truth communicated to us through our body or heart, and act accordingly. These moments can be as short as sixty seconds or composed of a significant life decision. Either way, we collect them. At first, even when trying, we will most likely not even recognize them. Then, gradually, we start accumulating them one by one, while also experiencing numerous unaligned moments in between. Moments of taking that extra bite, of saying or thinking something we later regret we ever allowed into our mouth or mind are still moments we can learn from. The motion of LOVE starts by recognizing unaligned moments, then growing into an accumulation of five soul moments a day. And if you have five soul moments, then you can have ten such moments, an hour, and then days.

Every moment with our children is an opportunity to walk more aligned with who we are. Our children bring to their journey issues related to us, or to one of the family members, asking us to resolve them together and heal them. They also bring many issues not related to us – issues they wish to resolve with other souls, in different places, ways, and times. As they grow, they need to set out on their journey and walk along the marks they set for themselves in the blueprint of their path, in their own scavenger hunt. Accordingly, grownups who, as children, receive the guidance of truth, attentiveness, and the motion of LOVE, and who walk in the world in congruence with their true self, have all the tools they need for walking life as they asked to in their blueprint.

For our children to have the tools to walk their true path, we must walk ours. We are one, and we are also each walking a unique path. There are no how-to's other than awareness and owning. Owning all details of our lives, from the lifestyle we choose to our behaviors, patterns, emotions, thoughts, and actions. The crafting of love within yourself – being attentive, walking truth, setting an example for your children, and creating the conditions for them to be who they are – is a personal journey as well as a family journey. Each of us contribute to the creation of our unique family walk of the LOVE that we all are.

If we did not receive such guidance as children, or if we forgot, we can still learn how to practice truth, attentiveness, and the motion of LOVE, even if it takes us a long time. It's never too late to begin. Four-and-a-half years after the car crash, my husband and I met a woman who had been severely injured in similar body parts. Seeing someone a few steps forward was very encouraging. At the time, I felt that after over four years, I should already be moving forward. But I had no idea what this progress was and what was to unfold. From her perspective, I was just taking my first steps. Four-and-a-half years after the car crash meant, for her, that I was no more than a month old. And more than ten years later, I understand what she meant and wonder: What will I feel, be, and see when I celebrate my fifteenth car crash birthday? And my twentieth? Deep healing takes time.

My personal train to the present stopped in many places, challenging and beautiful, frustrating and expansive. I had to learn to receive. To let those who loved me extend a hand. I had to learn to be weak so that others would have a place to care for me and bring forward their strength. I had to feel. I had to learn to work with what I had lost, as even with the most optimistic of natures, acknowledging what was left behind was what allowed me to move forward. I had to accept not knowing what tomorrow might bring. I had to learn to embrace uncertainty, to let it open opportunities and trails that I would have never taken otherwise. I had to embrace my strength and my ability to see beyond the ordinary. I had to experience deep forgiveness for myself, as well as for the other woman in this story.

We met by coincidence. Well, the word *coincidence* is not a fitting word for this book, as there are no coincidences. We met unexpectedly. It was the first time I drove alone. My daughters and I were at my mother's, and I had a physiotherapy session. It was raining, and I did not want my mother to have to take my daughters with her to bring me there, so I decided I was going to drive the two-minute distance on my own. I was both terrified and proud. And after the session, I decided I could go into the nearby neighborhood mall and get my sister-in-law a birthday present. I knew exactly what I was going to buy. I calculated the distances and felt I would manage to walk them, and I knew where there were benches where I could rest on my way. As in unforeseen curves, I went into the first store, a clothing store right at the mall entrance, and immediately found the perfect gift. It all went so well, so I decided to check whether they might have something for me, too. My body shape had changed so much. I tried something on and then went to look in the mirror. I described to the store owner what I was looking for. At the time, I was barely able to stand, and I explained that I had experienced a serious car crash about a year earlier. A woman trying something on in the other dressing room said she, too, had been in a car crash about a year ago.

Then she came out, looked at me, and whispered, "I think we are from the same story."

I was not sure if I wanted to hug her or strangle her, and I actually said that to her. While the police had found her responsible for the crash, within me I understood this is an earthly perspective. Eventually, after a loaded conversation with me sitting on the floor, as I was too weak and stunned to stand, I hugged her. It felt like a scene from a movie. Our meeting at the mall left us both shaking, confused, and in tears. I could not stop crying for many days. The meeting opened a gate within me that I was unaware I had closed and invited a release of intense emotions I had unconsciously held inside.

Three years later, after we had both walked a few steps forward in our healing journeys, and I was already starting to embrace the gifts brought by the integration of my physical reorganization and NDE, we scheduled to meet at a cafe. The minute we met up, I knew I loved this soul. It was an irrational feeling, LOVE that felt contrary to any logical, Earthly way of thinking. Although the police had deemed her responsible, the crash had happened for both of us. It could have easily been the other way around. I always feel that if a soul is willing to be the one who pushes you to move and shift, even if it seems to be in a very inconvenient way and at its own expense, like the other woman did for me, that is an amazing act of LOVE. So, from my heart to the heart of the other woman from my story: Thank you for stepping into my life.

Our life journey is less about the story of what happened than it is about the gifts that story brings. Writing is a significant gift this journey has brought. In my school years, I never did well in grammar. I learned how to write in an academic style while studying for my Ph.D., but I never thought I would be writing such a book or have a content-based website. Writing evolved from journaling for myself to some soul writing, then to little bits I shared with my email list, up to the writing of this book. And yes, it took years. Writing first gifted me with a way to communicate with myself. It gifted me with this process of forming coherent thoughts about my absentee parenting, and of finding the way to be the mother my daughters chose. More than anything, writing freed me from my story by turning it into an understanding and sharing it to facilitate others' connections to their own parenting quest.

When I got stronger, listening within and participating in life, I gradually noticed that I sometimes sensed things that were not just for myself. The NDE opened many gates to invisible dimensions of our world. This connection brought me enormous healing that bubbled into all layers of my being. In addition, as I connected to Spirit, to my higher guidance, I found I could mediate energetic healing for others. It surprised me, and I resisted it for a long time, until, like many other elements of our lives since the car crash, my need to explore it overcame my fears.

Our energetic field is a world we can know only by our own experience, an experience anyone who wishes to can have. My NDE was a significant facilitating force; however, it was an invitation I still needed to say yes to. And then another yes, and another. Today, I know that if someone wishes to, the experience of other dimensions can happen in many other ways. I found myself training in modern shamanism, and for a while, practicing shamanic energy healing and facilitating shamanic journeying groups for mothers and daughters. Who would have thought? It is a path of so much beauty, of a deepening connection to our Earth, to the elements, to every human being. It is a humbling path that has taken me to places I did not dare to dream of. To the possible. It is an example of where soul moments can take us, even when we do not know the destination.

Energy healing, the connection to my higher guidance, journeying, exploring the mythical aspects of other dimensions, and writing brought the gift of stories, like the ones I shared with you at the beginning of every chapter in this book. These stories come to me in simple shamanic journeying. I see an image, and it develops into a short tale. Mythical stories carry healing. They take us beyond time, into those deep parts within us that connect to the symbolic. They speak to us at the level of our soul's journey and guide us not in words, but in images and through our hearts, inspiring us to expand beyond the mundane and walk life with a broader perspective. I am touched by each story that evolves in front of me, and they are all part of the abundant list of blessings brought by the car crash and NDE, shared with you here. The word *gratitude* is too small for what this feeling holds.

More than ten years ago, the way our lives look now was not even something that came to me in my wildest dreams. When I was lying injured in the hospital and later recovering at home, it was impossible not to believe the doctors who continuously tried to lower our expectations. Most of them promised nothing and said, "It is not certain that you will be able to walk – we will have to see" or, "It is not certain that we will be able to close the stoma or that the intestines you have left will heal." Only one physician allowed himself to constantly propose a positive future outcome. These vague, uninformative descriptions of what was ahead accompanied us at all stages of my recovery. First, it was burdensome and confusing. Then, more and more often, we managed to ignore them. Today, I know that my body will never be as it was before. Still, I am not sure this is a bad thing. It has reorganized. It is in great shape compared to even the positive doctor's predictions. It is what it is.

I keep stretching the limits again and again. I can walk more than I ever dreamed I would be able to. I can even go on short hikes with my family. Sometimes, my left foot or other parts of my body scream after a few steps, and I send my family forward, finding a patch of shade in which to wait for them and meditate. The connection with nature is always worth not managing to move for a few days. Sometimes, I enjoy my quiet time at home, truly happy for my family, while they go on adventures beyond my abilities.

I choose to listen to all the signs my body communicates to me. I continuously watch what I eat in an attentive way. I have learned that when I avoid gluten, dairy, and sugars – foods that make me feel physically bad – I gain a clear mind. A brain fog I walked with for years, unaware it was even there, disappeared. A few years after the car crash, we realized that all our daughters are also sensitive to gluten, dairy, and refined sugars. I tend to think that food sensitivities are a way for our souls to guide us through our bodies to watch what we eat and eat only what nourishes us. And in this way, we are encouraged to remain connected to our source and the energy that we are and that which surrounds us. Our family journey with gluten and dairy-free nutrition brought us to create together an illustrated gluten-free, vegan cookbook for children. It was an enjoyable shared project, one that will hopefully support many children in listening to their bodies' request to avoid such food, either by a medical diagnosis or by choice.

Physical and soul healing go together. In my journey, I was invited to heal by both the crash and the NDE, which took place together, beyond time and at the same fracture of linear time. I own my walk and do everything within my power to heal any soul aspect that arises. I listen to my physical body's requests to rest and stop. We communicate. Me, my soul, my body. I know that any discomfort – physical, emotional, or mental – is always telling me something deeper, informing my being, inviting me into another layer of healing. It is an ongoing process with mostly forward movement. Yet, sometimes, my limited body slows me down. But even when the slowdown is frustrating, it is also always a significant gift. When I slow down, I listen. When I listen, I pay attention, and I am attentive to my truth. When I am attentive to my truth, I am aligned with my essence. I am joyful. I live Heaven on Earth. Here, within my physical presence. The more I am attentive, the more my daughters are. The more I listen, the more they listen, and the more we all walk many soul moments, together living more and more of our days in joy. Whole joy. That of true beings.

Times are changing. The transformation is much greater than we can grasp in our everyday lives, in our dense human perception. As part of these transformational changes, we are all, parents and children, invited to clear many energies we've collected throughout our lifetimes. To shed all that does not serve us anymore. We are encouraged to bring resolution to as many issues as possible and become ourselves, our essence. As part of these changes, many of us may experience the open gates between worlds, but not merely through NDEs. Many of us will experience it in various spiritual journeys, healing modalities, or shamanic work, all of which invite us to acknowledge the changes taking place on our planet and adjust to them.

Many of our children are agents of these changes. Their gates to other dimensions of reality are open and wide, offering them guidance and inviting us to resolve and shift with them – to connect back to the essence of LOVE that we all are. It is common to think that only a few children are children of light – sensitive, intuitive, empathic – who will bring such changes. But I have never met a child who was not a child of pure light when they were born. I have met children whose light I slowly and sadly witnessed becoming hidden, turned off, or sometimes even lost, turning into dying embers. That is where we parents come in – accepting and adjusting to changing times, accepting the invitations our children bring to us, embracing parenting as a journey of growth. Doing what we each must, finding our unique way to return to our path and be who we are. And thus, we can allow our children to remain the LOVE that they are. And if it is part of their path, they will be able to bring their service to Earth, to be the agents of change they intended to be.

My journey was and still is a journey of accumulating soul moments. It is a journey of learning to be LOVE. It is about learning to love myself, something I need to do from the very start of every day, every moment, as I am never the same person I was yesterday. It is a journey of learning genuine gratitude. Gratitude that comes deep from my heart. Gratitude to all those who walked and continue to walk this journey with me: my daughters, my husband, my parents, and my extended family, my amazing friends, my teachers, and my community. Having support when going through a crisis makes an enormous difference. I would have never reached these lines, learning to love, finding the way to live Heaven on Earth, full of joy and gratitude, without them.

Daily, as I hug my daughters, my heart explodes with gratitude. Gratitude for the souls they are. Gratitude for them choosing my husband and me as their parents. For believing that I would take that extended hand of the universe and become the mother they chose to come to, which I constantly try to be. Gratitude for the mere ability to be present in their lives. Yesterday. Today. Tomorrow. As we all grow together. Gratitude for the amazing humans they are all growing up to be. Gratitude for the moment. Gratitude for life. I am their mother.

Our hearts know. Our children's hearts know. They steadily invite us on the journey. It never seems easy. There are always so many excuses. Yet, the further we walk our journey, the lighter we become. Even when the road is bumpy, steep, and challenging, or the elevation challenges us with its decrease in oxygen. Even when we deal with a severe crisis, or if we are injured, sick, or disabled. Our hearts know. And the more we walk by the truth it communicates to us, the clearer the path becomes. Walking soul moments leads us forward and turns us into the creators we are. Sometimes inviting us to soar far from everything we ever thought we knew, and all becomes LOVE. Go out and start your journey, and if you've already started, then continue straight ahead. Trust the truth you know. Let your heart show you the path. You will most likely find your children are walking with you. They, too, promised to LOVE.

A Note To Readers

Dear Reader,

Thank you! You have read this far, and I thank you for that. First and foremost, I am grateful because I feel that if you choose to read my story, and even more, to open your heart to the deeper layer of what our parenting is about, it means that you care. Not all people do. I wish everyone did.

Wherever you are in your journey, I hope that what I shared with you reveals new fields of understanding and new ways for your relationships with your children to develop and soar. For you and your child, for you and your family, to reciprocally dance together, both being teachers, guides, and students.

I would be grateful to hear your story and what thoughts you welcome into your life after reading mine. You can find me through my website: www.efratshokef.com.

My website is also where you can download (free...) the book's workbook and audio versions of the journeys I offered you along the book, subscribe to my newsletter, read related articles, and learn about courses and workshops.

If you found the book and the ideas I shared worthwhile, please consider sharing your thoughts, inspiration, what you liked about it, or the one sentence that resonated with you. Your comments on your preferred platform can increase the book's visibility and assist other parents in consciously choosing whether this book is for them.

Thank you.

In blessings of Truth, Attentiveness, and in the Motion of Love,

Efrat

Acknowledgments

How do I recall and mention all the numerous amazing souls who walked with me, guided me, held my hand, embraced me, and encouraged me in the journey of creating this book? I will surely miss many, and in trying to avoid writing a whole book of gratitude, I will probably fail to capture my deep feelings... please know that my gratitude is above and beyond the listing (or not) of your names.

I am grateful to the countless paramedics, physicians, nurses, physical therapists, and others who saved my life and to the healers who guided me in crafting its quality. Deep gratitude to the community of heart-centered humans we live in. Thank you for all the little acts of kindness that made sure we could concentrate on my healing.

Thank you, Samara Bel, Liron Vacksman-Reuven, Nirmala Nataraj, and Shannon Azzato Stephens, for your invaluable comments, questions, teachings, challenges, and contributions to the development, writing skills, and editing at various stages of composing this book.

Adina Shelly, thank you for helping me hold the space behind the scenes and for our eternal friendship.

Marianna Pestana, thank you for believing in *The Promise We Made* and helping me make it happen.

Hindy List and Olga Belousova, deep, heartfelt gratitude for reading and encouraging me in the early stages of shaping this book.

Berta Kühnel, Lynn Berryhill, Marie-Claire O'Sullivan-Moore, Rita Pirkl, Karen Johnson, and Jenny Mannion: Thank you for being my teachers, writing allies, and colleagues on this beautiful, unexpected path I found myself gratefully walking.

My clients, all of you, and especially the children and teens, I am beyond honored to be walking with so many of you worldwide as my teachers. I hope we, adults, can create the conditions you need us to, and I know we will witness your beauty and gifts.

Keren Ungar, Noga Prat, Tanya Gilboa, Dana Shira, Hila Sekeles, Shirli Bel, Ella Mendelson, Michal Baron, and many, many others: Thank you for our shared walk. It is amazing to dance life with such soul friends; I am blessed.

Tali, the other woman in this story: Thank you for gifting me the transformation I needed and for our eternal evolving friendship.

My parents, Irith and Itamar: I chose well. May our journey together continue to evolve and support our mutual growth. I love you always. Judith, I am grateful for your love and belief, and to all three of you for being beyond amazing grandmothers and an extraordinary grandfather to your granddaughters.

Yair, my best friend. My partner in growth and adventures. This book would not have come to life, and my life could not have been nearly as fulfilling, joyful, and loving without you in it.

Yaara, Hadas, and Dafna, thank you for choosing us as your parents. Thank you for nudging me, and us, again and again to leap, trust you, and trust ourselves, and for growing to be such extraordinary humans. I couldn't have asked for better partners in the exploration of life. I am your mother.

About the Author

Efrat Shokef holds a Ph.D. in Social- Organizational Psychology and is a Fulbright Alumni. She embarked on a profound journey into the essence of motherhood and parenting after a near-fatal car crash and simultaneous Near-Death Experience.

As a devoted mother, prolific writer, captivating speaker, nurturing teacher, and empathetic healer, she passionately guides children, teens, parents, and families to embrace their soul's path.

Efrat is the mother of three spiritually aware and intuitive teenage daughters who constantly inspire her to grow. She is a wife, daughter, sister, friend, cosmic journeyer, and writer. Efrat homeschools her daughters, raises four loving dogs, and enjoys spending time outdoors, reading, and cooking.

Explore Dr. Shokef's transformative insights at www.efratshokef.com.